THE MANKIND SERIES OF GREAT ADVENTURES OF HISTORY

THE AMERICAN INDIAN

THE MANKIND SERIES OF GREAT ADVENTURES OF HISTORY

THE AMERICAN INDIAN

Compiled, edited and with an Introduction
by Raymond Friday Locke

A Mankind Book

MANKIND PUBLISHING COMPANY
LOS ANGELES

CONTRIBUTORS

"History, Red Power and the New Indian," by Raymond Friday Locke, © 1970 by Mankind Publishing Company.

"The End of the Anasazi," by Robert Silverberg, © 1970 by Mankind Publishing Company.

"The Pueblos of New Mexico," by Walter Jarrett, © 1968 by Mankind Publishing Company.

"The Trail of Tears," by Lillian Morris and Philip Procter, © 1970 by Mankind Publishing Company.

"The Peace Messiah," by Sharon S. and Thomas W. McKern, © 1970 by Mankind Publishing Company.

"Humor of the American Indian," by Robert Easton, © 1970 by Mankind Publishing Company.

Library of Congress Catalog Card Number: 76-135908
SBN: 87687-003-5

Book design by Andrew Furr

CONTENTS

HISTORY, RED POWER AND THE NEW INDIAN

by Raymond Friday Locke

*I*nstead of the usual introduction, I'm taking the liberty of reprinting an essay of mine that appeared in the September, 1970, issue of *Mankind* which was very well received by both Indians and concerned whites. In this short piece I have attempted to explain to the uninitiated white what Red Power is about and to point out that the first Americans were not "uncivilized savages" prior to their exposure to European culture.

At this writing the Indians have taken over Alcatraz and are doggedly holding onto it with the hope that it will be given to them by the government as the site for an Indian cultural center. The Paiutes of Nevada have organized to keep whites from destroying their Pyramid Lake and the Taos Indians of New Mexico are insisting, rightly, that the government give them free title to 40,000 acres of land that has always belonged to them considered holy land by that tribe.

Jeanette Henry, a Cherokee of San Francisco, has founded American Indian Educational Publishers, the first publishing company organized and directed by American Indians. Indian parents are refusing to send their children to "Indian" schools. The Navajos have formed their own college, a school run by Indians for Indians and a second Navajo reservation school is rewriting Indian history—this time from the Indian point of view. There have been three excellent books published on Red Power recently and a Kiowa-Choctaw, N. Scott Momaday, has won the Pulitzer Prize for his *House Made of Dawn.* And most white Americans are sitting about looking at each other and asking, "What's it all about? What do *they* want?"

What they want is self-respect. They don't want to continue to be taught how to be white and they're, with good reason, tired of a government which has systematically eradicated their self-respect. And they want whites to stop thinking of them as a subspecies; savages that had to be all but exterminated to make America safe for good white Christian settlers.

Alcatraz is but a symbol, a symbol that has helped unite Indians against the whites after four hundred years. Columbus was welcomed by the Indians of the West Indies with open arms. He repaid them by immediately sending five hundred of their number to be sold into slavery in Spain. The others were not so fortunate. Within ten years after the whites reached Puerto Rico the Indian population of that island had been reduced by ninety percent. Hispaniola Indians met the same fate. But the United States had nothing to do with *that*, a white might say.

The record of the United States is worse than that. The United States government signed the first Indian treaty with the Delaware tribe at Fort Pitt in

1778—and broke it a few months later. And, for the record, a large group of Delawares, by then good Christian Indians, were brutally murdered a short time later, by whites, after they had been removed from their ancient homeland to Ohio by the government—for their own protection.

Over the next ten decades the United States Senate ratified 370 treaties with various Indian nations and Father Washington's army turned right around and broke virtually every one of them—usually to protect poor defenseless settlers, who'd just happened to take up residence on Indian lands, from "savage redskins."

As a case in point, take the example of Andrew Jackson and the Choctaw nation of Mississippi. The Choctaws always fought (albeit foolishly) on the side of Father Washington. They joined up with Andy Jackson to fight the Creeks and joined his forces again to help him win fame and glory at the Battle of New Orleans in the War of 1812. Soon after that conflict the Choctaw nation signed the Treaty of Doak's Stand in which they gave up thousands of acres of their land (I suppose they figured they might as well as long as white settlers were living all over it anyway) and were promised by none other than Andrew Jackson that "pegs would be driven, lines marked, never to be obliterated" and the Choctaws could live on the remainder of their Mississippi land forever.

A few short years later, after he'd gotten himself elected president, Andrew Jackson rammed the Indian Removal Act through Congress and signed it. This act forced the Choctaws from their green Mississippi hills to Oklahoma. For a sampling of what Jackson did to the Cherokees read "The Trail of Tears" in this book.

Then there was the Navajo treaty of 1868. Father Washington got tired of feeding the Navajos at Fort Sumner where he'd forcibly removed them four years earlier from their ancestral homeland and told them if they'd go back to their old hunting grounds and behave themselves he'd give them sheep, and a teacher for every thirty Navajo children. The government finally got around to replacing the Navajo sheep which had been systematically killed in the 1864 war but about those one-for-thirty teachers, forget it . . . which was just as well. Most of the ones the Navajos did get were hopeless misfits and desired only to teach the Navajos how to be white and to take up the white man's religion.

Then there was the matter of the Plains Indians. That was easy. As a matter of *policy* the army killed off the buffalo, which resulted in starvation as a "final solution" to the Plains Indian problem.

When confronted with these facts, I once had a historian at one of the nation's larger universities say, "but those people were *savages!*" Were they?

The entire field of American Indian history must be—and is being—subjected to a revolution in spite of passive resistance from the conservative academicians. In light of recent archaeological evidence the old dogmas no longer apply and must be discarded—and will be once historians stop thinking of archaeologists and anthropologists as undesirable step children. For example, some secondary school textbooks are still giving space to that old lie that the ancestors of the American Indians crossed a Bering Strait land bridge about 10,000 years ago. Two Indian histories published in 1969 state irrevocably that the ancestors of the American Indians arrived in the Western Hemisphere no earlier than 10,000 years ago in spite of the fact that we have had evidence to the contrary for almost half a century.

Well into the twentieth century historians were convinced that the first Indians arrived in America about the time of Christ. The Spaniards of the sixteenth century and the Mormons of the nineteenth century were convinced that the Indians were the lost tribes of Israel. Dozens of theories as to who the Indians were and where they came from were advanced and entertained for varying lengths of time. At one time or another it was thought that the American Indians were descended from ancient Greeks, Egyptians, Carthaginians, Etruscans, Tartars, Chinese, Africans, Irish, Welsh, Norse, Basques and Huns, who either migrated to America intentionally or whose ships were blown off course.

There was, of course a land bridge connecting Alaska with Siberia not only during the last glacial (Wisconsin) stage of the Pleistocene epoch but at other times as well. Historians have found it expedient to say that the ancestors of the American Indians crossed over from Siberia to Alaska on this land bridge and let it go at that. But that is not the total answer any more than is Dr. Daniel Wilson's hypothesis of a peopling of the New World by Polynesians or the Bolivian etymologist Vallamil de Rada's theory that the Indians are indigenous to America.

Actually the Bering Strait has been a continuous pathway between the Old World and the New for at least 30,000 years and possibly twice that long. Today only fifty-six miles of water separates the continents of Asia and North America and halfway between are the Diomede Islands, steppingstones from one world to the other. Even now, when the Bering Strait freezes over in the winter, it is possible to walk from Alaska to Siberia and, until the U.S.S.R. forbade it, Eskimos from Alaska and Siberia freely visited and traded back and forth across the winter ice.

While man entered America through the area of the Bering Strait just as the horse—a true American native—in turn entered Asia long before his descendants became extinct in the New World (and actually re-entered America only to become extinct a second time), there is evidence of many contacts with peoples of other cultures. The earliest white explorers to the American northwest coast not only found Indians that looked Chinese but also found them in possession of brass Chinese coins. Pottery found in Central America is identical to Japanese pottery of the same period and there is considerable evidence that Europeans visited the east coast of America long before Columbus.

It wasn't until 1926 that the prescribed doctrine of a recent peopling of the New World received its death blow, and it came about as the result of the curiosity of a Negro cowboy named George McJunkin. While searching for some lost cattle near the little town of Folsom, New Mexico, McJunkin came upon some gigantic bones along with several stone points that had once been spear tips. In the scientific investigation that followed it was learned that the bones belonged to Taylor's bison—an animal that had been extinct for at least 10,000 years. Embedded in the remains of the longhorn bison were nineteen of the spear tips. Further investigation revealed that man—now known as Folsom man—had ranged wide and hunted Taylor's bison from Canada to Texas 10,000 years ago.

The discovery of Folsom man eventually led to the discovery of the Llano or Clovis culture. Clovis man used a distinctive spear point and the Clovis points as well as other artifacts associated with the culture have been found from Alaska to Mexico and in every one of the contiguous states. He proceeded Folsom man by at least two thousand years.

Finally, in 1936, archaeologists discovered traces of a still earlier man in a cave in the Sandia mountain range east of Albuquerque, New Mexico. This race was named Sandia man and from the bones he left behind beside his long-ago campfires we know that he was hunting the horse 25,000 years before the Spaniards reintroduced it to New Mexico.

Ten millennia before Christ, the American Indian developed the faculties for killing mammoths and followed that beast wherever he wandered. Twelve thousand years ago he hunted caribou in what is now New York; he inhabited a cave in southern Illinois, lived on the shores of a long-forgotten lake in California's Mohave desert and hunted in the woodlands of Alabama. He followed his prey down through the Isthmus of Panama to the southernmost tip of the New World where, in Fels Caves in Tierra del Fuego, Chile, he roasted the flesh of camels and horses over his campfire 10,720 years ago and left the bones to be dated by Carbon 14 tests in the twentieth century.

Indians were cultivating corn in central Mexico 6,000 years ago—three millennia before the bow and arrow, an Old World invention, made its appearance in America.

At about the time, or shortly after, Roman Emperor Octavius Augustus charged architect Marcus Vitruvius Pallio with rebuilding Rome, American Indians—probably the Aymara—in Bolivia embarked upon a building program that would have staggered the imagination of those proud Romans who found Rome a city of clay and left it a city of marble.

South of Titicaca, 13,000 feet above sea level in the Andes, these Indians built a city called Tiahuanaco that rivaled, if not surpassed, anything in the Old World at that time—including Rome. Mining massive blocks of stone that weighed as much as one hundred tons, they transported them several miles over mountainous terrain and, without the use of mortar, fitted them to a precision and exactness in cutting, squaring, dressing and notching that amazes architects even today. But the Indians who built Tiahuanaco not only excelled in architecture, they were masters of the art of ceramics and Tiahuanaco painted pottery is one of the great achievements of pre-Columbian art.

The tales of dozens of other Indian tribes such as the Maya, Toltecs, Incas and even the Aztecs, whose capital, Tenochtitlan, was said by Cortes to rival the splendor and size of Venice, could be related here. The evidence that the Indian has been in the Americas a very long time and that many tribes reached a very high level of "civilization" which at least equaled that of the white civilization of Europe of the same period cannot be denied. It can be said that the Indians often only become "savages" in order to survive after their contact with Europeans.

Now the Indian is fighting back. Alcatraz has focused attention to his plight. He has discovered at long last that he has a history and a culture and that it is important to preserve what he can of that history and culture. And finally, united, he may be able to keep his Pyramid Lake, his property and his rights—and without giving up his cultural heritage.

THE LEGEND
OF THE
WHITE GOD
AND THE
CONQUEST
OF MEXICO

by Ronald Leal

*T*he legend of a bearded white god who would return to them one day was prevalent among many of the Indian tribes of pre-Columbian America. The Hopis, living in what is now northeastern Arizona, knew the white god as Pahana (One from across the Water); to the Mayas of Central America he was known as Kukulcan and to the Aztecs of Mexico he was Quetzalcoatl.

The Aztecs, or *Mexica*, were borrowers of culture and their legend of Quetzalcoatl (the Feathered Serpent) came down to them from the Toltecs, who preceeded the Aztecs to prominence in Mexico by several centuries. Quetzalcoatl was not only the god of light and learning, he was also the patron of agriculture, civilization, and that virtue singularly lacking among the Aztecs, humility. When the Aztecs came from the

*Cortes taking leave of the governor
of Cuba, Diego Velasquez*

north and conquered the Valley of Mexico and subjected the descendents of the Toltecs, they incorporated Quetzalcoatl into their theology. (Oddly enough there is some reason to believe that the Aztecs were migrants from the Anasazi cities of New Mexico and Arizona. According to their legend, they began their wanderings in 1168 or about the time that Chaco Canyon was deserted and spoke a language similar to that spoken by the Hopis of Arozona.)

According to legend, Quetzalcoatl had descended from heaven, assumed mortal form, brought his subjects learning and civilization and tried to persuade them to stop the practice of human sacrifice which he considered evil. The latter angered the principal, and older, diety of the Aztecs (and also of the Toltecs), Texcatlipoca (the Mirror that Smokes) who demanded sacrifice so that the sun would make its way across the heavens each day and Quetzalcoatl, the man god, white of skin and black of beard, was driven out. He and his court boarded a raft on the coast near Tabasco and headed eastward, promising to return in a One Reed year (Ce Acatl) to re-establish his rule.

Prophecy plays an uncanny role in the arrival of the Spanish *conquistadores* among the Aztecs for 1519 was a One Reed year. Preceding One Reed years, which occurred every fifty-two years, the Aztec priests and astrologers were particularly attentive to omens and signs from the heavens that would signal the return of Quetzalcoatl. Such signs, in the form of earthquakes, floods, strange dreams and a brilliant comet with a large tail which was seen in the sky for several nights running, came in abundance in the year preceeding 1519. Nezahualpilli, the king of Texcoco, came to Montezuma, the high king of the Aztecs, after observing the comet and told him of a dream he'd had: "Terrible, frightful things will come . . . in all our lands and provinces there will be great calamities and misfortunes, not a thing will be left standing. Death will dominate the land!" (from *The Aztecs,* Fray Diego Durán, New York: Orion Press, 1964). About this time messages of a somewhat more immediate, if less divine, emergency came to the king of the Aztecs in the form of reports from the Gulf Coast of strange men who had landed at Tabasco and Champoton in large floating castles. Mystic and priest-ridden, Montezuma chose to become frightened out of his wits over the former and all but ignore the latter. But he did send emissaries to investigate the strangers who returned and reported that they had seen men with white skins and black beards, dressed from head to foot in hard metal and carrying weapons of the same material. These were, of course, the heralds of Quetzalcoatl!

Actually these strange white men were the expedition led by Juan de Grijalva, sent out by the governor of the newly discovered island of Cuba, Diego Velasquez, to explore the area to the west, in April, 1518. The governor had sent an earlier expedition, under the command of Francisco Hernandez de Cordoba in February, 1517, which had found the coast of the Yucatan and fought and lost a battle with some unfriendly Mayas. The Cordoba expedition managed to escape the Mayas but did capture some gold ornaments which, of course, prompted the second expedition. The Grijalva expedition followed the same course taken by that of Cordoba, encountered more unfriendly Mayas but, instead of returning to Cuba, turned north for farther exploration. At Tabasco the Grijalva party encountered some very friendly Indians who spoke a language different from that of the Mayas. These natives were quite amenable to trading and gave the Spaniards gold in return for glass beads. Quite without realizing it, Grijalva had traded beads for gold with the emissaries from Montezuma, completely ignorant of the existence of the latter or of the vast inland empire he ruled that,

in many ways both culturally and artistically, far surpassed anything the Spaniards had ever known—or
dreamed could exist.

But within a matter of years it would all be reduced
to dust and the city of Tenichtitlan, where Montezuma now awaited the return of his emissaries and their
report of the white strangers, would furnish the building blocks for Mexico City, the city of the Spaniards
and their capital of the Western World. From Mexico
City the Spaniards would, within two decades, launch
their conquest of the American Southwest.

Much has been made of Cortes' conquest of Mexico
with only 553 soldiers pitted against the army of
150,000 or more at Montezuma's disposal but the true
story of the conquest of Mexico is infinitely more complicated than a mere matter of comparing the size of
the two armies. At the time Grijalva was making his report to Governor Velasquez—a report that prompted
the governor to outfit a new and larger expedition—
Montezuma, true to his nature, was doing absolutely
nothing but listening to the contradictory advice of a
horde of vassels none of whom, by law, could look upon
his face, and worrying about where he should hide if the
prophecies of Nezahualpilli should come true. Instead
of going about the very urgently needed task of tight-
ening the reigns of his "empire," he occupied himself
with securing a new sacrificial stone, one that would reflect the grandeur of Mexico, as he considered the
stone his grandfather had set up too small and too
cheap!

In Cuba, meanwhile, Governor Velasquez was busy
assembling ships and stores for the new expedition and
trying to find a captain-general that he could trust to
head such an important expedition. He did not find a
man he could trust but he did find Hernando Cortes.

Born at Medellin, Spain, in 1485, Cortes was the son

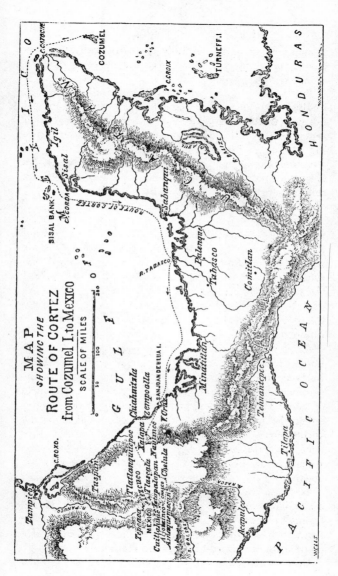

Map showing route of Cortes

Cortes in battle against the Mayas

of a poor country gentleman. He studied at the University of Salamanca for two years, then returned home restless and without a vocation. In 1504, at the age of nineteen, he arrived in Hispaniola and 1511 found him serving under Diego Velasquez in the expedition that subjugated Cuba. Once in Cuba he acquired considerable land holdings and became, by local standards, a rich man.

In spite of the strong support Grijalva attracted, Cortes began to promote himself as the leader of the third expedition. He had become both popular and influential in the Cuban colony and as Velasquez began to ready the four ships from the Grijalva expedition and to arrange for six more to join the fleet, Cortes used all the influence he could muster to intrigue—and bribe—his way into the command of the new expedition to the west. For whatever reasons—because of his political influence or for personal reasons—Velasquez passed up the more qualified Grijalva and gave the appointment to Cortes. But the governor had second thoughts about the appointment even before the expedition was underway. When Cortes learned that the governor was thinking of replacing him, he outmaneuvered Velasquez by ordering his officers, sailors and soldiers aboard the ships and sailed to Trinidad to continue preparations. Velasquez sent a messenger to the mayor of Trinidad to relieve Cortes of his command but the message came too late. Fired with enthusiasm, Cortes had already won the loyalty of most of his men in spite of the fact that some of his officers were relatives and friends of the governor. As the mayor of Trinidad stood by and timidly watched, Cortes sailed on February 10, 1519, with 506 swordsmen, 100 sailors, 32 crossbowmen, 13 musketeers, 16 horses, several brass guns and four falconets. Now in his thirty-third year, Cortes was a handsome man of medium stature and, like most Spaniards of his day, eager to take the cross to the heathens in return for their gold.

Cortes followed the course of the Grijalva expedition and fought his first battle at Tabasco. The Maya Indians bravely stood their ground against the firearms but the sight of the horses was too much for them. Believing the horse and rider to be one, a beast from another world, the Mayas turned and fled. Meanwhile a stroke of luck had thrown a most valuable asset into the hands of Cortes. At Cozumel, while taking native prisoners in search of an interpretor, he found the Indians repeating one word over and over—*Castilian*—the name the Spaniards used to refer to themselves at the time. Presuming, correctly, that the natives had learned the word from a Spaniard, Cortes sent boats to the mainland in search of European castaways on the shores of Yucatan. They found Jeronimo de Aguilar, who had been shipwrecked on the coast eight years before. Cortes not only had an interpreter—but a Spanish interpreter.

Cortes took Tabasco, hacked three slashes in the trunk of a large tree and took possession of the land in the name of King Charles I of Spain. Twelve days later the Spaniards fought their second pitched battle against the Tabascans on an open plain near the town of Cintla. Again the horses frightened the Indians and again the Indians were routed, with a loss of eight hundred men. Cortes lost two.

The Tabascans capitulated and brought the Spaniards gifts of fish, birds, fruits, golden ornaments, dogs, ducks and a number of slave women, one of which turned out to be more valuable than gold. The Spaniards named her Dona Marina and, as she was not only highly intelligent but beautiful and spoke both the Maya language of the coastal Indians and the Nahautl language of the Aztecs, she soon learned Spanish and became Cortes' chief interpreter—and his mistress.

Five days later Cortes sailed up the coast into Mexican territory and landed at the present port of San Juan

*The interview between Cortes and
the Aztec nobles*

de Ulua. In the Christian calendar it was Good Friday, April 22, 1519. In the Aztec calendar it was Nine Wind Day of One Reed Year—the exact date on which Quetzalcoatl was expected to return to the Aztecs.

Cortes was met at San Juan de Ulua by a large party of Indians who came in peace to inquire as to what manner of men they were. Emissaries from Montezuma, they returned to Tenochtitlan and reported that, indeed, white men with black beards had come from the sea and had landed on the coast on Quetzalcoatl's day.

The local Indians, believing that Cortes was Quetzalcoatl and that the Spanish soldiers were all, in fact, *Teules*—gods—were won over without a fight. Too, these people, the Totonacs, were a subject people to the Aztecs and like all the Aztecs' subjects had, in recent years, been taxed almost beyond endurance by Montezuma's extravagance and his incessant demand for sacrificial victims to soothe his religious fanaticism. And therein lies the story of how Cortes and his few followers were able to conquer the most powerful people of the Western World. Cortes arrived in Mexico at a time when the Aztec subjects—who overwhelmingly outnumbered the true Aztecs—were at the point of revolution for a reason as old as time: Excess taxation. Cortes furnished the stimulus for the revolt of the Aztec subjects much as the Boston Tea Party furnished that for the American Revolution. The fact that Montezuma was a mystical tyrant whose sense of self-importance had long since caused him to lose sight of reality as well as the affection of his people helped pave the way; his hesitation in coming to a decision as to whether Cortes was or was not the god Quetzalcoatl made the conquest a certainty from the beginning.

From San Juan de Ulua, Cortes moved to the mainland and built a base of operations which became the present-day city of Veracruz. Then he set about putting his own house in order. For some time the relatives and friends of Velasquez in his party had shown an eagerness to return to Cuba and re-establish themselves with the governor, whose power, after all, was recognized by King Charles. Gathering up all the gold and other presents that had been given him by the various chiefs and by the ambassadors of Montezuma, Cortes outfitted the largest ship in the fleet, loaded it with treasure and provisioned the vessel for the voyage to Spain and the court of Charles I. Only the king could make the final decision as to who was to command the Spanish forces here. Choosing fifteen sailors and two officers whom he trusted, Cortes sent them off to Charles I with the treasure which he hoped would sufficiently impress the king not only as to the promising prospects of this new land but also to the abilities of Hernando Cortes. Once his emissaries had sailed, Cortes stripped his fleet of iron, sails, cord, and equipment and burned it to the last ship. The followers of Velasquez would now remain and conquer with Cortes whether they liked it or not. Then he set off to take a look at this great city of *Mejico* (Tenochtitlan) of which he had heard so much. It was August, 1519.

The town of Tlaxcala was located roughly halfway between Veracruz and Tenochtitlan. The Tlaxcalans, a fiercely independent people, rejected the Spaniards' peace overtures, thinking this strange new army to be in the employ of Montezuma. For three weeks Cortes, who had brought along about five hundred Spanish soldiers, thirteen horses, several pieces of light artillery and a force of about one thousand Totonac irregulars, stormed the Tlaxcalan capital. After three major battles the Tlaxcalans sent an embassy to the Spanish camp, proposing terms of peace. More than fifty persons bearing rich presents composed the embassage. Cortes suspected them, perhaps with good reason, of merely acting as spies and immediately ordered their hands to be cut off. The cruel deed was promptly executed and the

*The Spaniards destroying the
Aztec idols*

sufferers, thus mutilated, were sent to their city with the defiant message that the Spaniards were ready for the Tlaxcalans whether they came "by day or came by night."

Now the commander-in-chief of the Tlaxcalan army, with a large retinue, entered the Spanish camp with proffers of submission. Cortes, aware of the great peril from which he had just escaped, with stern words, but with secret joy in his heart, accepted the submission and entered into a cordial alliance with Tlaxcala—and gained his most valuable ally. The Tlaxcalans, a militant people, had maintained their independence in spite of constant Aztec onslaughts, despised the Mexicans and, once they lost the battle to the Spaniards, immediately became their friends in the hope that these foreigners could help them do what they had never been able to do alone—destroy the Aztecs. Not only did Cortes now have the Aztecs' most powerful enemies in his camp, he was daily growing more attractive to the Aztec subject peoples by doing exactly what Quetzalcoatl would have done, by damning that most cherished of rituals demanded by the Aztec diety Texcatlipoca: human sacrifice.

Meanwhile Montezuma was alarmed by the victories of the foreigners and sent five of the most conspicuous nobles of the empire, accompanied by a retinue of two hundred attendants, to see Cortes. They brought with them the most costly gifts of Mexican manufacture as well as considerable gold and the request that Cortes cease in his march toward the Mexican capital. Cortes replied that he must obey the commands of his sovereign, which required that he visit the capital of the great Aztec empire.

While resting at Tlaxcala, the Spaniards were presented, among other gifts, with a number of beautiful girls. Since the Christian Spaniards could not marry heathens (indeed, most of Cortes' officers had left wives behind in Cuba), the Indian girls were promptly baptized. One of the girls, the daughter of Xicotencatl, the high chief of the Tlaxcalans, was given by her father to the Spanish general Alvarado. Her descendants would become important throughout the history of Mexico.

Montezuma, finding that he could not dissuade Cortes from his march and fearing an enemy wielding seemingly supernatural powers, now endeavored to win his friendship. He sent a second embassy to Cortes at Tlaxcala, bearing even more costly gifts, and inviting the Spaniard to his capital. But he warned him not to enter into any alliance with his foes, the Tlaxcalans.

Cortes took up the march toward Mexico, his army swollen by six thousand Tlaxcalan volunteers. At Cholula, a beautiful city containing, according to the chroniclers of Cortes, a population of one hundred thousand, the Spaniards were received with the warmest tokens of cordiality. But upon noting that many of the streets had been barricaded, piles of stones were visible on the rooftops and, most ominous of all signs, that there were no women and children to be seen anywhere, the Spaniards became suspicious. The faithful Marina, ever on the watch, detected, as was supposed, a conspiracy. The Cholulans, in league with Montezuma, were planning to ambush Cortes' army and carry it to Tenochtitlan for sacrifice. Cortes contrived to ambush the Cholulans first and asked the unsuspecting Indians to assemble in the public square, which they did along with all their high officials. At an appointed signal, Cortes' soldiers and his allies opened fire from the surrounding rooftops and other stations and a storm of destruction was swept through the helpless throng. The pavements were almost instantly covered with the dying and the dead. Everywhere they turned the Cholulans were met by missiles of lead, iron and stone. By Cortes' own estimate, more than 3,000 men died in the next two hours.

*The massacre of the Indians
at Cholula*

The first view of Tenochtitlan

The Tlaxcalans took countless women and children prisoners. Cholula, with its wide, neatly arranged streets and spacious stone houses, was sacked and burned. Cortes, with less than 350 of his Spanish troop left, but with his Tlaxcalan allies following him, marched out of Cholula.

The Aztec cities had been built on four large lakes which comprised one vast inland sea. The capital, Tenochtitlan, stood on an island off the western shore of the largest lake, Texcoco, and was connected to the mainland by a series of causeways, each of which was equipped with defensive drawbridges. Years later Bernal Diaz del Castrillo wrote his impression upon first sighting Tenochtitlan: "We saw many cities and villages built in the water and other great towns on dry land and that straight and level causeway going toward Mexico . . . we were amazed and did not know what to say. Some of our soldiers asked whether the things we saw were not a dream . . . there were things that had never been seen before or heard of, not even dreamed about."

It was fifty miles from Cholula to Tenochtitlan, a march that led the conquistadores up between the twin volcanoes southeast of the City and through a pass 12,000 feet high. Along the way vast crowds turned out to see the Spaniards but Cortes, relying upon the efficiency of gunpower and the cross, marched on. Montezuma, ever indecisive, sent another embassy to Cortes, offering him four loads of gold and one for each of his captains and a yearly tribute to the king of Spain if he would turn back. This message delighted Cortes for it was an indication of the weakness and fear of Montezuma.

On November 8, 1519, Cortes led his army along the southern causeway toward Tenochtitlan and was met by a party of Aztec nobles who announced that Montezuma was on his way to meet Cortes and welcome him to his capital. There, on the causeway, the Old World and the New came face to face: "The great Montezuma descended from his litter, and the other great chieftains supported him beneath a marvelously rich canopy of green feathers, decorated with gold, silver and pearls. And there were other great Lords who walked before the great Montezuma, laying down cloaks so that his feet should not touch the earth. Not one dared to raise his eyes toward him."

The emperor's address of welcome made a strong impression on the Spaniards. He greeted Cortes as a king and a god and seemed—at least to Spanish ears—to be offering the Spaniard the throne of Mexico. The strangers were then escorted into the city and installed in apartments prepared for them. Montezuma left to consult his gods and stall for time. And Cortes did exactly the same thing. Throughout the following week Cortes and Montezuma conversed and the latter showed the Spaniard about the magnificently beautiful city which had a population estimated at no less than two hundred thousand and possibly as high as half a million. Cortes neither admitted nor denied being the god Quetzalcoatl but he did remain steadfast in asserting that he was a vassal of the great king across the eastern waters, Charles I, which, no doubt, perplexed Montezuma greatly. Until now he had been the king of kings and here this white creature who might be the god Quetzalcoatl was telling him that he, himself, was the vassal of even a greater king who ruled over many other kings!

Meanwhile the Spanish soldiers wore their armor day and night, maintained a strict guard at the palace Montezuma had put at their disposal and kept their horses at ready at all times.

In the weeks that followed the Spaniards grew to like and respect Montezuma who, according to Bernal

*The first meeting of Cortes and
Montezuma*

Diaz, was tall, slim and had eyes that were at once tender and grave. But one aspect of the Aztec capital repulsed the Spaniards and that was the great temple where humans were sacrificed. Bernal Diaz wrote: "The walls of (this) shrine were so caked with blood and the floors so bathed in it, that the stench was worse than that of any slaughterhouse in Spain." Montezuma listened to the talk of the Spanish god; he had seen many examples of their cruelty and could not understand their revulsion to human sacrifice.

Then, when a fight broke out between the troops that Cortes had left at Veracruz and a Mexican force which resulted in the death of the Spanish commander, Juan de Escalante, and several of his men, Cortes went to Montezuma's palace, accompanied by a body of his soldiers and put the surprised emperor under house arrest.

Meanwhile, in Cuba, Velasquez had put together a new expedition of nineteen ships and about 1400 men and sent it out under the command of Páufilo de Narváez to kill or capture Cortes and his band. When he received the word that the Narváez force had landed at Veracruz, Cortes left eighty men, under the command of Pedro de Alvarado, to hold their position in the capital and marched off to meet the new threat. Cortes overcame the Narváez force, mostly by tempting the new troops with examples of the great treasures that could be had for the taking in this new land—and thereby increased his force by a thousand men, fresh horses, powder and arms. He had Narváez's ships beached and stripped to make sure word of the deed did not get back to Cuba, and started back to the capital.

But in Tenochtitlan disaster had struck. During an annual May religious festival Alvarado had suddenly suspected a plot against his garrison. Leading his men into the temple precinct, Alvarado ordered every Indian present killed. More than a thousand Indians, including the flower of the Aztec nobility, were slaughtered. Within the hour the entire city was up in arms and the Spaniards were blockaded in their palace. Montezuma intervened and there was no further bloodshed. Montezuma's position was already a precarious one and by extending his protection to the invaders he brought about his downfall. On the very evening that Cortes returned to Tenochtitlan, a specially convened Aztec Council of State deposed the emperor from his throne and selected his first cousin Cuitlahuac to rule in his place. By morning active hostility had replaced the passive sullenness of the past days. Cortes, not knowing that Montezuma no longer held any power over the populace, called upon him to speak to his people. Montezuma protested, telling Cortes that there was nothing he could do. But he finally agreed to make one final effort. He donned his robes of state, stepped out onto the terrace above the great square and began to speak. But his person was greeted by a hail of stones, one of which struck the former emperor on the head. The Spaniards carried him inside. Three days later he was dead. While Cortes has been accused of killing the emperor as he had no more use of him, Cortes himself, in a dispatch to Charles I, said: "One of his subjects hit him on the head with such force that within three days he died. I had his body taken out by two of the Indian prisoners but I do not know what his people did with him."

The Aztec capital was now an armed camp, surrounding the Spaniards. What if Cortes was Quetzalcoatl? Had not Texcatlipoca driven the Feathered Serpent from the city once before?

That night Cortes, with his Tlaxcalan allies, made a daring escape from Tenochtitlan. Slipping silently from their quarters and beginning their march along the western causeway—which was shorter than the south-

The fall of Montezuma

The battle of the causeway

ern one—they were surprised. by the alert Aztecs. Cortes lost many men (not a few who drowned because they were weighed down with stolen gold), most of his horses, muskets, crossbows and all of his cannon. Captives, Spaniards and Tlaxcalans alike, were led to the sacrificial temple. In the Spanish tradition Cortes' escape from Tenochtitlan has come to be known as *la noche triste*—the Sad Night.

Cortes led the remnants of his army toward the safety of Tlaxcala but four days after their escape from Tenochtitlan they were intercepted at Otumba by a Mexican army. In the battle that followed on July 14, 1520, the Spaniards avoided capture only by killing Serpent Woman, the Mexican commander-in-chief and sending the Aztecs into retreat. The Spaniards then marched on to the land of their Tlaxcalan allies, where they rested for five and one-half months and where Cortes prepared for his return to Tenochtitlan, by constructing a fleet of thirteen shallow-draft brigantines, specially designed so that they could be dismantled into easily portable sections and reassembled on the shores of Lake Texcoco. Between August and November several ships put in at Veracruz with men, horses, and munititions. Some of the ships had been sent by Velasquez as reinforcements for Narváez as the Cuban governor had not yet learned of his defeat. Others were traders but they all became a source of new men and supplies for Cortes. When Cortes left Tlaxcala to march on the Mexican capital on December 28, 1520, his army consisted of 450 Spanish foot soldiers, a cavalry of over forty, nine field cannon—and 10,000 Tlaxcalan warriors as determined as ever to kill the Aztecs to the last man.

Upon reaching the valley of Mexico, Cortes drove the Mexican garrisons from the towns around the lake, which caused the towns to ally themselves with the Spaniards. Next the water line from Chapultepec to

Tenochtitlan was severed which left the Mexican capital with no source of water except for the few wells in the city (Texcoco was a salt lake). Then Cortes divided his army into three units and stationed each of them on one of the causeways giving access to the city and, finally, he launched his thirteen brigantines which, aided by allied canoes, cut off ship contact between the city and the outside world. Cortes had cut off all food and water supplies to Tenochtitlan. And inside the city a strange new malady, introduced by the *Teules*,—yellow fever—raged, claiming as one of its first victims Cuitlahuac who was succeeded by Montezuma's nephew Cuauhtemoc.

Cuauhtemoc refused to negotiate with Cortes, no doubt remembering the fate of his uncle, in spite of the fact that his people were starving and, according to Diaz, visiting the Spanish camps at night to beg for food and water.

Daily the forces of Cortes and the Aztecs fought on the causeways, with the Spaniards gaining bit by bit until they were finally in the city. Once in the city Cortes ordered his men to systematically destroy the houses and streets one by one. By the end of July, when the southern half of the city lay in ruins and the southern and western spearheads of the Spanish attack—led by Cortes and Alvarado—met in the great marketplace, the conquest was all but over. The shrines were set on fire, the idols were destroyed and for three days and nights those who were still alive and able streamed out of the city, over the causeways, in search of sustenance until few but the aged, the sick and the dying were left.

Twenty-six year old Cuauhtemoc refused to surrender but was captured attempting to escape. The few holdouts ceased fighting. But much to the disappointment of the Spaniards, the young emperor had cast the treasures of Tenochtitlan into Lake Texcoco. Much to

49

The capture of Cuauhtemoc

Cortes' disgrace, he allowed the man who had so nobly led his people to be tortured and finally killed and with him died the pride of the Aztecs.

Tenochtitlan furnished the building blocks for the Spaniards' Mexico City. By the time a decade had passed very little of it that was Mexican remained.

The city of Mexico and environs

THE END OF
THE ANASAZI

by Robert Silverberg

*O*n a lofty plateau in the southwestern United States is the only point in our land where four states—Arizona, New Mexico, Colorado, and Utah—meet. Known as the Four Corners country, it is a spectacularly beautiful region of prairies, mountains, deep gorges, eroded terraces, and steeply rising mesas. Cliffs of bright red sandstone sparkle in the hard clear sunlight.

It is dry country, though not nearly so dry as the Arizona-New Mexico desert to the south, and not nearly so hot. Even at the height of summer, the daytime temperatures are comfortable; at night there can be a sharp chill, for much of the area is more than ten thousand feet above sea level. Where the land is high, it is covered with a forest of stump piñon pines and gnarled junipers; in the lowlands, gray-green sagebrush spreads over mile after mile, dotted with clumps of yucca and beargrass.

Here the great Pueblo Indian culture of the Southwest began. An ingenious, stubborn band of farmers settled here, living first in caves and shallow pits, eventually building the grandest prehistoric cities of the United States. They left behind the great ruins of Mesa Verde and Chaco Canyon to mark their presence on the land; the Indians of today's twenty-five surviving pueblos are their descendents. Archaeologists often call these ancient city-builders the *Anasazi*: a word from the language of the Navaho, late arrivals in the Southwest, that means "the Old Ones."

The oldest of the Old Ones were the basketmaker people, who came to the Four Corners country about two thousand years ago. Possibly they were desert-dwellers from Utah or Nevada; perhaps they drifted up from the cactus lands to the south. In the Four Corners regions they found what seemed to them to be a friendly environment. They had just enough water to let them raise corn and squash, and along the steep canyon walls there were shallow caves in which they could take shelter.

They were farmers, more or less. Their small, clumsily tended fields provided enough food for survival. The caves that were their homes were hardly more than niches, open to the sun and wind. Where caves were not to be found, they built crude brush shelters. They did not yet know the art of making pottery, but they fashioned excellent watertight baskets from yucca fibers.

In time they abandoned the caves, moved to open ground and began to build small villages. By about A.D. 500 they were living in pit-houses, round or oval, two to five feet deep and nine to thirty feet across, covered with sturdy roofs of mud-plastered timber and reeds. They became potters; they grew new varieties of

The Anasazi ruins at Chaco Canyon were abandoned
nearly eight hundred years ago, yet many walls still stand.

corn, with bigger ears than the earlier kinds, and added such high protein foods as beans to their crops.

About 700 A.D. the most enterprising of the Anasazi villages experimented with a new sort of dwelling, entirely above ground, with upright walls and flat roofs. Within two centuries, these rectangular houses were being built in rows up to fourteen units long. They were structures of poles and mud at first, then of stones, embedded in mud, and ultimately of neatly squared slabs of sandstone set in adobe mortar. It became possible to add a second story on top of the first. Villages took the form of double-tiered rooms, arranged either in a crescent or a straight row.

The pace of progress quickened among the Anasazi. The villages grew larger, the architecture more sturdy. New concepts evolved as Anasazi culture spread. The heart of the civilization still was the Four Corners country, which had three main centers of Anasazi life: the Mesa Verde area of southwestern Colorado; the Chaco Canyon district in northwestern New Mexico; and, in northeastern Arizona, the vicinity of the modern town of Kayenta. Less advanced groups sharing some of the Nasazi traits could be found in such outlying areas as Utah, southeastern Nevada, and the Big Bend country of Texas.

In this time of expansion corn remained the basic food. The ears could be stored like stacked logs after the harvest, and the dried kernels ground into meal as needed during the months that followed. Beans and squash were still the important secondary crops. The invention of the stone hoe made cultivation easier and produced a bigger yield of food. Anasazi hunters, armed with bows and arrows, brought back bear, elk, buffalo, wolf, mountain sheep, and other game.

The villages—which we know by the Spanish term, "pueblos"—underwent radical transformation. The basic unit remained the rectangular room built of stone slabs mortared with mud and roofed with poles and brush, but now these units were added together to form great compounds, some with hundreds of rooms. This was the most impressive structural achievement of any Indian civilization of the United States. At Chaco Canyon, at Mesa Verde, and at hundreds of other Four Corners sites, towering pueblos were constructed, enlarged, modified, repaired—and ultimately abandoned in a tragic evacuation.

We can set extremely exact dates for the construction of these huge "apartment houses," thanks to a method known as dendrochronology, or tree-ring dating—perhaps the most precise system of archaeological dating yet devised. It was developed by an astronomer, not an archaeologist: Dr. Andrew E. Douglass, who died in 1962 at the age of 94.

At the beginning of this century Douglass was studying sunspots at Arizona's Lowell Observatory. Seeking some correlation between the eleven-year cycle of sunspot frequency and weather on earth, Douglass was hampered by the lack of reliable weather reports prior to the eighteenth century: Who had kept weather charts five hundred or one thousand years ago?

As he rode through a forest of tall ponderosa pines near Flagstaff, Arizona, he thought of the growth rings of trees. He knew that each year a tree adds a new layer of wood over its entire living surface. Seen in cross-section, the annual growth pattern appears as a series of ever-expanding rings. In a wet year the ring is broad; in a year of drought it is narrow, since a tree grows less if it lacks nourishment.

Beginning in 1904, Douglass began to analyze cross-sections of ponderosas from the Flagstaff area. The trees averaged 348 years old, according to a count of rings. The width of the outer rings corresponded with local rainfall records of recent years. Moreover, the same patterns could be found in every tree. Familiar sequences emerged: perhaps three wide rings followed by two narrow ones, a wide, two more narrows, two wides, three narrows—a year-by-year record of drought and rainfall.

By 1915 Douglass had pushed his analysis of tree-ring patterns back far beyond the earliest precipitation records. By collecting specimens from the giant sequoia trees of inland California he was able to extend his observations three thousand years into the past. Though his basic interest was in the sunspot cycle, Douglass found himself becoming deeply involved in Southwestern archaeology. Since the oldest living pines in the Southwest were only about 640 years old, he turned to the Pueblo Indian ruins, hoping to add to his record of tree-ring patterns by examining ancient logs and timbers that had been used as building materials.

From his sections of living trees, he had plotted a graph that showed him the relative width of tree-rings for the years from 1300 to 1916. He could compare a section from any living pine of Arizona or New Mexico with his master chart and discover when that tree had begun growing. And he could point confidently to certain rings on his chart to show that the Southwest had, for example, experienced droughts in 1379 and 1672.

In 1916 the American Museum of Natural History allowed Douglass to examine some sections of pine logs from Pueblo Bonito in Chaco Canyon and from the ancient ruined pueblo near Aztec, New Mexico. Three years later he visited the ruin at Aztec and took fifty samples from house-beams. Thus he was able to develop a new chart covering some two hundred years. None of the ring-patterns on this chart corresponded to those on his chart of six-hundred-year-old living trees. That told him that the logs at Pueblo Bonito had been cut some time before 1300. But how much earlier?

Douglass called this prehistoric chart his "floating

chronology." If he could tie it to his living-tree chronology, he would not only gain much information about ancient weather patterns, but would provide a startlingly accurate tool for dating pueblo ruins.

Archaeologists provided extensive cooperation. Douglass received more specimens from Pueblo Bonito and added 150 years to the floating chronology. From the Mesa Verde ruins came other samples that matched neither the Pueblo Bonito chart nor the modern chronology. Douglass suspected that the Mesa Verde rings went somewhere between, in the mysterious gap, but at the moment they simply gave him a second floating chronology.

In 1928 timbers from an Arizona ruin supplied a pattern that linked the latest rings of the Pueblo Bonito chronology to the earliest ones of the Mesa Verde chronology, joining the 350 years of the first to the 180 years of the second. The new floating chronology now covered more than 580 years in continuous prehistoric sequence.

In the same year a National Geographic Society expedition visited the Hopi Indian villages of Arizona, which had been continuously inhabited since the fourteenth century. Douglass went along and after lengthy efforts at persuasion won permission to drill simple cores in the oldest-looking ceiling beams. In an abandoned house in the village of Oraibi he found a sample that gave a clear series of rings fitting into his modern chronology and carrying it back forty more years, to A.D. 1260. The log had been cut about 1370, Douglass found.

Even now, however, the modern chronology could not be linked to the prehistoric floating one. Douglass suspected that the gap was unlikely to be large. The Oraibi sample indicated that there had been a great drought late in the thirteenth century. The Mesa Verde sample revealed the thin rings of drought at their late ends. Douglass now followed a trail of archaelogical clues to solve his problem. The Hopi, it was clear, had come to Oraibi early in the fourteenth century, just after the time of drought. Where had they lived previously? If the site could be found, it might yield a beam that joined the chronologies.

A comparison of pottery types showed that the Hopi migration route had passed through Arizona. In 1929, at the small Arizona town of Showlow, Douglass drew from an ancient pueblo his missing rings. The pueblo had been destroyed by fire centuries ago, but Douglass had developed techniques for reading the tree-rings even on a bit of charred, blackened wood. One fragile, badly burned log seemed to hold the key. The outer end of this beam—designated Beam HH39—showed the now-familiar rings of the fourteenth century.

Douglass followed inward—1380, 1350, 1300. Now he came to the time of the great drought. He wrote a few months later, "Here were the very small rings that told of the hardships the tree had endured in 1299 and 1295. As we studied the rings further toward the center, 1288, 1286, 1283, and 1280 each told the same story we had found in other beams of lean years and hard living."

The drought rings continued back to 1275. The rings beyond them matched those of the Oraibi beam. That one ended in 1260 but HH39 went on and on—1254, 1251, 1247. "Finally," Douglas wrote, "came the one at the very core and from its central ring we learned that this charred old stick began its life as a promising upright pine, A.D. 1237, just ten years after the Sixth Crusade moved eastward to compel the Saracens to restore Jerusalem."

Late that night, under a sputtering gasoline torch, Douglass labored to link his chronologies. Beam HH39 had carried the modern chronology back another twenty-three years, to 1237. He turned now to the floating chronology. Its 551st ring matched perfectly with that of the ring for the year 1251 in Beam HH38. The gap no longer existed. Douglass now knew that his floating chronology began in A.D 700, and that its final worn and defective rings actually overlapped with the earliest rings of his Oraibi beam.

Everything fell into place. His oldest Pueblo Bonito timber had been cut in 919, from a tree 219 years old. An important section of Pueblo Bonito had been built in 1067, and the pueblo still had been occupied in 1127. The ruins of Kayenta, Aztec, Mesa Verde, and other Anasazi sites could be assigned precise, accurate dates. His discovery was a landmark in archaeology.

Tree rings tell a detailed story of the rise and fall of the great pueblos, and of the environmental forces that buffeted the diligent farmers who built them. In New Mexico's Chaco Canyon, for example, sprawling buildings occupy a somber desert. Between the irregular red sandstone walls of the canyon lies a broad, parched plain more than a mile wide, sandy and forlorn. Tough, scraggly desert plants live here: sagebrush, saltbush, greasewood, rabbitbrush. No trees are in sight. Tiny ground squirrels scurry across the sand.

Yet nine centuries ago this valley swarmed with busy men and women. In what is now a barren waste of sand and rock, bitterly cold in winter and fiercely hot in summer, more than a dozen great pueblos were built. A visitor in the year 1000 would have seen men at work in green fields of corn, women squatting before their houses, artfully shaping vessels of clay, naked children chasing one another through the broad plazas, pet dogs barking and pet turkeys gobbling. Chaco Canyon throbbed with life.

Then everything changed. The clouds no longer dropped life-giving rain. The stream that was the source of life for the Chaco folk went dry. The fields of corn shriveled. The villagers moved away. Under the

Anasazi ruins in Canyon de Chelly, Arizona

merciless eye of the sun the stone buildings crumbled and collapsed and were covered with drifting heaps of hot sand. Chaco Canyon became a land of the dead, bone-dry, fit only for lizards and sagebrush.

The toppled pueblos remain as a sign of vanished greatness. Today five of the dozen most important Chaco ruins have been excavated completely or in part. The rest are as time has left them: shapeless weed-covered mounds, out of which jut leaning stone walls. Pueblo Bonito is the grandest—a breathtaking sight, even in its present ruined state. It is D-shaped, with the curving belly of the D close to the cliff wall, and the backbar looking south across the canyon. That straight south-facing wall is 518 feet long. Behind it lies a great open plaza, and beyond was the main section of the pueblo, terrace after terrace of rooms that rose in ancient times to a height of five stories.

The entire pueblo covered three acres and contained some eight hundred rooms. It housed as many as twelve hundred people. For centuries Pueblo Bonito was the largest apartment house in the world; it was not surpassed until the building of the Spanish Flats in New York City in 1882. (The Spanish Flats are gone, demolished to make way for still bigger buildings. Pueblo Bonito remains.)

The oldest section of Pueblo Bonito dates from about A.D. 900. The pueblo's masonry is of several styles showing successive expansions; the earliest work is quite crude, but later sections are elegantly constructed and archaeologists believe they represent the work of a distinctly different group of Anasazi who took over the existing pueblo. Tree-ring dates show that construction ended at Pueblo Bonito in 1130. A migration from the pueblo began; many upper rooms were abandoned and allowed to collapse; stubborn hangers-on inhabited the lower sections for another twenty or thirty years, and then they, too, were forced to leave.

One theory has it that the Chaco folk were harassed by fierce nomads, the ancestors of the Navaho and Apache Indians. These tribes came originally from the far north; the evidence for this lies in their language, which belongs to the Athabascan group of languages spoken by the Indians of western Canada and Alaska. The Navaho-Apache dialect is closely enough related to the dialects of the north to permit an Arizona Navaho to carry on an understandable conversation with a caribou-hunting Indian of the Yukon, even though centuries have passed since the Navaho came south.

We do not know when the nomads of the north first reached Anasazi country. Pottery of a kind made by certain Athabascan-speaking tribes has been found in Gobernador Canyon near Aztec, New Mexico, in association with tree-ring dates of 710-875 A.D. There is evidence of fire destruction at this settlement, so perhaps it was ransacked by an advance party from the north. The identification is still unsure.

The next nomad invasion seems to have come about 1100. Archaeologists working in the Colorado Rockies have found circular stone buildings resembling the *hogans*, or domed lodges, that the Navaho build. And Athabascan-like pottery has been found—again associated with burned pueblos—at several minor Anasazi sites. Although no evidence of Athabascan raids on Chaco Canyon has been unearthed, it is possible that some nomad harassment was felt there.

However, the main reason for the abandonment of Pueblo Bonito seems to have been environmental. The canyon was growing dry and barren. From 1090 to 1101, the tree-rings tell us, one year of drought followed another at Chaco. The crops withered. The Anasazi had themselves altered the Chaco environment for the worse. When they had arrived, thick stands of pine and fir grew in the canyon; but they had been felled by the thousands for the roof beams of Pueblo Bonito and the other huge structures. The timber found in the pueblos showed no scars indicating it had been cut a great distance away and hauled to Chaco. It was local wood.

When all the trees of the canyon were gone, no root systems remained to slow the rush of flood waters in the wet years. Now the spring torrents came sluicing through the canyon, scouring away the fertile topsoil to expose bare rock. The floods cut a deep arroyo, or gully, through the new treeless valley. It became the only channel for the water that once had swirled over the entire canyon floor to bring life to the fields. Beyond the arroyo's edges the shrubs and grass died of thirst and, with the ground cover gone, the flood run-off became even more violent.

Bewildered by the rapid transformation of their fertile valley into a desert, the Pueblo Bonito folk moved elsewhere in the Four Corners region. Perhaps a dozen families still lived in the great pueblo by 1150, paralyzed by fear, victims of the marauders who entered Bonito again and again.

The other Chaco pueblos, some nearly as majestic as Bonito, were being abandoned now, too. Late in the eleventh century, at the height of its glory, the canyon had had a population of thousands; but by the middle of the twelfth century all its pueblos were virtually deserted.

While the exodus from Chaco was going on, one band of Anasazi seems to have moved *into* the canyon. They came from the north, from the Mesa Verde country, and built a pueblo west of Bonito. It is known today by the Navaho name of Kin Kletso. It is totally unlike the other Chaco pueblos, which are large and sprawling, centering around big open plazas. There is no plaza at Kin Kletso; the building is small, compact, forbidding-looking. It has yielded tree-ring dates as late as 1178, almost half a century later than those of the neighboring pueblos.

Archaeologists have pictured these latecomers building their town as a fortress against the nomad raiders, and settling down every night after hauling up their ladders, leaving no access to the doorless walls of the ground floor. But a time came when these people had to leave Chaco, too—almost certainly because of climatic problems, rather than trouble with nomads—and when they were gone, the valley fell silent.

One of the places the Chaco people went was Aztec, some sixty miles to the northeast. It is poorly named, for there never were Aztecs here; the name, born of ignorance in the nineteenth century, simply persisted until it became permanent. Aztec was built quickly, between 1110 and 1124; it is a well-planned village, three stories high in some places, with masonry of the high quality associated with the latter-day work at Chaco.

But the builders stayed at Aztec less than a generation; about 1130 they moved on to parts unknown. There could have been no shortage of water at Aztec, situated near the Animas River, and no tangible evidence of nomad raids has been found, so possibly some religious reason, unfathomable to us, compelled the people of Aztec to abandon their new and solidly built pueblo. For a full century Aztec stood empty, until about 1225 wanderers from the Mesa Verde areas in the north moved in, rebuilt the pueblo in their own style, and occupied it until about 1300.

The tree-ring record shows a severe drought in the Southwest from 1276 to 1299, and this quarter century of sparse rain must have played its part in pushing the second occupants of Aztec toward new territory. Drought alone would not have forced the Anasazi from Aztec, but there were other hardships. Fire broke out in the east wing of the pueblo and destroyed many rooms. Those who were left homeless evidently preferred to migrate rather than to rebuild. There may have been nomad troubles.

When the people left, it was a quick departure. They sealed all doors and windows as though they planned to return, and wished to protect the things they were leaving behind. But no one returned until explorers found the ruins in 1859.

The great drought of the late thirteenth century had particularly heavy impact on the major Anasazi center of Mesa Verde in the heart of the Four Corners. The entire sequence of Anasazi dwelling types can be seen at Mesa Verde, from primitive pit-houses to large pueblos. While the giant Chaco buildings were being constructed, these northern folk were erecting smaller apartment houses in somewhat the same style.

After Chaco had been abandoned, the Mesa Verde people began to build pueblos of a new type, which cannot match those of Chaco for size but which have such otherworldly grace and splendor that they have become the most famous Anasazi dwellings. These are the cliff-houses of Mesa Verde: castles in the sky, airy villages nestling in shallow niches high above the canyons.

Until about 1200 the Mesa Verde people lived on their mesa-top plateaus. Evidently under pressure of enemy attack, though, they took a drastic defensive step by moving to great high vaults in the sides of cliffs, protected by huge stone overhangs but open to the sun. These caves were not deep—it might be no more than sixty or seventy feet from the rim of a cave to the back wall—but they were so high and broad that they could contain an entire pueblo.

So the strange and wonderful cliff-houses were built. Some were big enough to house hundreds of people; others had no more than three or four rooms. In every cranny of the Mesa Verde cliffs the new houses rose, always in hard-to-reach places whose trails needed only a few warriors to guard. But the cliff-houses of Mesa Verde were inhabited only a short while. In one brief, furious century of building, scores of the lofty, romantic dwellings were constructed, and then were abandoned.

By 1300, hardly anyone remained. The Four Corners country, ancestral home of the Anasazi, was left behind, and the Old Ones headed south and east and west to new lands, new homes—some to Arizona to found the Hopi villages, others into New Mexico to settle in the valley of the Rio Grande.

Why did the Anasazi leave? The tree-ring tale is grim: almost no rain at all fell from 1276 to 1299. Lean harvests, springs running dry, trees withering in the canyons, and always the mocking smile of the cloudless blue sky. An entire generation was born and came to adulthood without knowing a real downpour.

Farming became a grueling battle against dryness. Water had to be rationed; women now walked for miles to bring full jugs from the nearest spring. Animals fled to greener pastures, cutting the game supply. Even the wild nuts and berries were hard to find. The men danced and chanted, begging the gods to send rain, and no rain came.

But the people of Mesa Verde had known drought before and it had not driven them from their homes. The tree-rings tell of dry spells lasting five years or more about 1170, 1218, 1237. Why did the Anasazi leave now? Was this drought so much more terrible than those of the past?

Perhaps wandering warlike tribes were invading Mesa Verde also—if not the ancestors of the Apache and Navaho, then some non-Athabascan trib. The cliff-houses themselves would have been safe from attack, but nomads rampaging on the mesa-tops could cut the

Anasazi off from their fields and springs.

Archaeologists have found little evidence of actual warfare in the Mesa Verde area, however, and no traces of Athabascans prior to about A.D. 1500. Yet that does not preclude such marauders; and possibly the combination of severe drought and frequent raids convinced family after family that the gods had withdrawn their blessing from Mesa Verde, and that it was time to seek new homes. A great trek began, and the outward flow continued for a full generation, until finally there was no one left.

The clans dispersed. The great communities of the Four Corners, proudest Indian settlements of pre-Columbian times in the United States, were no more. parched ruins alone remained at Aztec, at Chaco, at Mesa Verde, as the great chapter of the Anasazi reached its end.

By the fifteenth century, the people we know as the Hopi were established on their mesas in Arizona, while the Rio Grande had gained the cluster of adobe villages that survive into our own times—Taos, Cochiti, San Ildefonso, Zuni, Santo Domingo, Jemez, Picuris, and more than a dozen others.

The old religions still thrive there. The old languages are spoken yet. Remorseless gods shriveled their ancestors' lives with drought seven hundred years ago, and drove them from their cities, but could not crush them entirely.

The twentieth century is rapidly enveloping these people, but still the old rites flourish. And the Anasazi way may withstand the onslaught of modern civilization after all. These are a people who have weathered drought and plague, famine and war. We who are newcomers to their land come among them to stare at their dusty mud-walled pueblos and their strange dances and at the sun-baked ruins of their former greatness, and we nod at the television sets and the shiny cars and tell ourselves that the Pueblo folk are becoming "civilized" at last.

But they have been civilized a long time. They have lived in their dry, harsh country for twenty centuries or more, and in that time they built a society that had no use for war, a society where every person was important, where the sick and aging were cared for with love, where family ties were always sacred. Out of the poorest materials, sandstone slabs or desert mud, they built great cities.

They are the Anasazi—the Old Ones. They have endured and survived. And they are still there.

The Zuni Olla Maidens of Zuni, New Mexico

THE PUEBLO INDIANS OF NEW MEXICO

by Walter Jarrett

*W*hile most of the American Indians have constantly changed—and have been changed—by a prolonged contact with the white man, the Pueblo Indians of New Mexico have stubbornly maintained their ancient culture. Their clans have continued to function and their social structure is largely intact.

The Pueblos were discovered in the 16th century by Spanish explorers in search of an Old World myth. Early in that century it was believed that in the New World would be found the fabled cities and creatures of which Europeans had heard for centuries—the fantastically rich Seven Cities of Cibola. The original discoverer of Cibola was supposedly an 8th century bishop of Lisbon who, fleeing from the Arabs, journeyed to islands in the western sea where he and his followers founded seven cities.

And when Cortes conquered Mexico the Indians there related to the Spanish explorers a bit of their folklore: they had issued forth from seven caves "in the north." The imaginative Spaniards soon related these seven caves to the famous seven cities of their own folklore. The first man of Old World blood to traverse the area where the seven cities were supposed to be located was Estevan, the Moor.

But the story actually began with Cabeza de Vaca. With two other Spaniards and the Moor, Estevan, he was shipwrecked and cast ashore in what is now Texas. They wandered west part of the way up the Rio Grande, and then south into Mexico. Cabeza learned the languages of the Indians he visited, as did the slave Estevan, and heard stories of fabled cities rich in gold, silver, and precious stones somewhere to the north. Falling in with other Spaniards who were catching Indians as slaves near what is now Culiacan, Sinaloa, they repeated the tales of the "Cities of gold."

Cortes had only recently taken golden plates as large as wagon wheels from the Aztec palace of Montezuma and already there were reports of cities of the Incas in Peru where even more gold had been found. Therefore, it was easy for the Spaniards to believe that the seven cities were indeed close at hand.

A friar, Marcos de Niza, was sent out in 1539 to find the seven cities and preceding him as scout was Estevan, the Moor. Estevan succeeded in reaching the town of Hawikuh, a village two and three stories in height inhabited by about 200 warriors, but the Indians slew him. Fray Marcos reported seeing Hawikuh, the first of the Zuni pueblos, from afar, but fearing that if he ventured nearer he would suffer Estevan's fate he turned back. Viewed from a distance, the rosegold adobe of a New Mexican pueblo in the light of the sun could very well appear to be made of gold. Certainly it did to Fray

Marcos (if he actually saw it) who quickly returned to Mexico with the news that he had at last discovered the Seven Cities of Cibola.

Fray Marcos' report led to the expedition of Franciso Vasquez Coronado, which began a three-century Spanish occupation of what is now New Mexico. Arriving in Hawikuh in July, 1540, Coronado fought the first of all Spanish-Indian battles in New Mexico. Pedro de Castaneda, chronicler of the expedition, wrote: "When they saw the first village, which was Cibola, such were the curses that some hurled at Friar Marcos that I pray God may protect him from them. It is a little, crowded village, looking as if it had been crumpled all up together. There are ranch houses in New Spain which make a better appearance at a distance . . . When they refused to have peace on the terms the interpreters extended to them, the Santiago (war cry) was given, and they were at once put to flight."

Coronado wrote of the battle for Hawikuh: "I ordered the musketeers and crossbowmen to begin the attack. They (the Indians) directed their attack at me because my armor was gilded and glittered. They knocked me down to the ground twice with great stones. If I had not been protected by the headpiece I wore, the outcome would have been bad for me."

The Zunis fled, overpowered by superior arms, leaving Hawikuh for the Spaniards who found houses not of gold but of adobe and "much corn, beans, turkeys and salt." But the Spanish thirst for gold was not so easily quenched. An exploring party was sent eastward and reached Acoma, then proceeded to Tiguex on the Rio Grande, and finally to the Pecos River. Leaving the main body of his expedition on the Rio Grande, Coronado pushed on, for he had been told by a slave who desired only to lead the invaders away from the towns of the Rio Grande that a land called Quivira lay to the north.

Coronado's expedition was a failure, so far as its main purpose was concerned. Other fabled "cities of Cibola" proved as disappointing as the first. No mines were discovered, yet they crossed country that would, later, prove extremely rich in minerals.

Forty years elapsed after Coronado before the Spaniards again entered the land of sedentary natives whom the Spanish called Pueblos (village dwellers) because of their compact, permanent settlements of stone and adobe. But long before, centuries before Coronado visited the land, they had been known as the *Anasazi—*the Ancient Ones—so named by the Navajos who entered the Southwest about or before 1200 A.D. These Ancient Pueblos were a people of considerable culture, surpassing that of Europe of the same period in many, if not most, ways. The *Anasazi,* probably because of a great drought, moved to their present-day pueblos at least 200 years before the second Spanish expedition, that of Fray Augustin Rodriguez who explored the Rio Grande valley in 1581.

In 1582-1583 Antonio Espejo made extended explorations of the Rio Grande valley, and it was about this time that the Spaniards in Mexico adopted the term New Mexico to designate the land to the north; Rodriguez had called the country San Felipe, and Espejo had named it Nueva Andalucia. Between 1583 and 1595 attempts were made to conquer and occupy New Mexico but, for various reasons, they were unsuccessful.

In the spring of 1598 Don Juan de Onate, under contract by the Spanish government to colonize New Mexico, entered the territory with about 400 colonists and built the town of San Francisco at the junction of the Rio Chama and the Rio Grande. The next year the name of the town was changed to San Gabriel. The pueblo country was then divided into districts, a priest assigned to each one, and the Indians were required to take oaths of obedience and homage to the Catholic Church and the Spanish Crown. Onate replaced the Indian names of the pueblos with those of Spanish saints —which most of them retain today.

In 1610 the Spaniards built *La Villa de la Santa Fe de San Francisco de Assisi,* now called Santa Fe, which has ever since been the seat of government of New Mexico. That same year Captain Gaspar de Villagra published his *History of New Mexico,* ten years before the pilgrims landed at Plymouth Rock and 14 years before the publication of Captain John Smith's *General History of Virginia.*

A "law of the Indies," issued in 1620, decreed that each pueblo select by popular vote a governor, lieutenant governor, and other officials to carry on pueblo civic affairs. As his symbol of authority, each governor was given a silver-headed cane topped with a cross.

By that date the Franciscan missionaries had built seven churches and had baptized 14,000 Indians. But the zeal of the friars in stamping out the religious rites of the natives, the severe punishment inflicted for non-observance of the rules of the Church, and the heavy tribute in kind demanded by the Spanish authorities aroused feelings of resentment in the pueblos and led to a general revolt in 1680, headed by a native named Pope.

Over 400 Spaniards were massacred and the remnant, after enduring a siege in Santa Fe, fled south to a mission near present El Paso, Texas. The Pueblos burned the churches, buried the bells and crucifixes, and shed their priest-given cognomens and called themselves by their old names. They even took soapweed baths to wash off the stains of Christian baptism.

For a decade the Indians enjoyed their independence, destroying all vestiges of Spanish occupation. After several attempts at reconquest had failed, Don

The Taos pueblo

Diego de Vargas marched up the Rio Grande in 1692 and, largely by moral persuasion, secured the province in the name of Spain. During the next four years the submission of the Indians was secured and the permanency of Spanish occupation was assured. The history of the next hundred years was uneventful, marked only by raids by the warlike tribes of Utes, Apaches, Navajos, and Comanches.

During the Mexican War of Independence (1811-1821) New Mexico was little disturbed by the events farther south. The Pueblos received the news of independence with enthusiasm as they expected their lot would improve under an independent government. While Mexico's Declaration of Independence did declare all Indians citizens on an equal basis with non-Indians, little changed for the Pueblos.

Following General Stephen W. Kearney's conquest of New Mexico for the United States in 1846 the Indians of the Taos pueblo, encouraged by their Mexican friends, revolted and on January 17, 1847, assassinated the governor, Charles Bent, and a number of Americans as well as several Mexicans who had aided the Americans.

Under the Treaty of Guadalupe Hidalgo, which ended the war between Mexico and the United States, an area which included New Mexico was ceded to the United States. Treaty articles provided for recognition and protection of Indian rights previously established under Spanish and Mexican rule. In 1849 the Bureau of Indian Affairs, until then a quasi-military service, was transferred from the War Department to the newly established Department of the Interior. James S. Calhoun was appointed first Indian Agent in New Mexico and in 1851 became the Territory's governor.

Pueblo lands were in question for many years thereafter, as Indian holdings were intruded upon by white settlers. In time the Supreme Court confirmed most of the tribally owned Pueblo lands outside boundaries of the original Spanish grants, and additional land patents were issued to individual Indians. The Enabling Act of 1910, which admitted New Mexico to the Union in 1912, specifically provided that ". . . the terms 'Indians' and 'Indian country' shall include the Pueblo Indians of New Mexico and lands occupied by them." In 1924 all Indians of the state were declared citizens of the United States, eligible to vote, and in the same year passage by Congress of the Pueblo Lands Act determined the status of Indian land claims and restored Pueblo holdings.

Today the Pueblos live in 26 towns, most of them near the upper Rio Grande in central New Mexico. To the east stand Picuris, Jemez, San Ildefonso, San Juan, Santa Clara, Nambe, Tesuque, Santo Domingo, San Filipe, Santa Ana, Chochiti, Zia, Taos, Sandia, and Isleta. West of these, but still in the Rio Grande drainage, are the pueblos of Acoma and Laguna. Farther west on the headwaters of the Little Colorado River is the pueblo of Zuni.

In northeastern Arizona, also in the drainage of the Little Colorado, stand the seven Hopi villages. In this same group is the pueblo of Hano, settled in early historic times by immigrants from the Rio Grande region. Despite a cultural homogeneity, no single tongue prevails among the various Pueblo towns. Zuni and affiliated villages, for instance, have one all of their own.

Today Taos and Zuni are the skyscrapers of Pueblo land. Taos dwellings reach five stories. Each of the five is smaller by the width of a room than the one below it, producing a rectangular terraced pyramid. At Santa Clara and Jemez, buildings face the four sides of a court, climb in terraces at front, and end with a perpendicular wall in the rear.

Sometimes buildings climb away from both sides of a street, as at Acoma. The upper tiers are entered by ladders projecting through holes in the roof, although now side doors are becoming common, as the danger of attack from nomad tribes and subsequent access to the pueblo no longer exist.

The strongest common factor remaining among the Pueblos today is religion. Although nominally Christianized, all Pueblos maintain—to a very great extent in some of the more conservative towns—their ancient beliefs. The complex Kachina cult remains an important feature of Pueblo social organization. Kachinas, according to legend, are spirits who brought rain and other gifts to the people, taught them to farm and hunt, to dance, and to make pottery and other utensils.

The Kachinas are nearly two hundred spirits who the Pueblos believe live beneath the waters. According to their religion, the Kachinas visit the village each year at which time they are impersonated by Pueblo men wearing costumes and masks. The Kachina dolls, often sold to tourists, have no religious significance but are used to teach children the names and functions of each Kachina, but Kachina masks are extremely sacred and are never sold or given away.

The Kachina cult is only one of several such cults in the Pueblo religion, each of which is dedicated to the worship of a particular set of supernatural beings. Pueblo religion—and the various cults—is very complicated and difficult for outsiders to understand.

A very religious Pueblo may spend half his waking hours engaged in religious activities; virtually everything he does is hedged about with religious strictures. Most religious celebrations are closed to outsiders, even, oftentimes, to other Pueblos who are not members of the particular cult.

It is in his religion, more than in any other way, that the Pueblo of New Mexico has resisted the influence of the white man—and change from his ancient ways.

THE TRAIL
OF TEARS

by Lillian Morris and Philip Procter

*T*he short, balding, bewhiskered man who stood before the Congress of the United States on December 3, 1838, carried himself with a dignified bearing that had often been lampooned by his vitriolic Whig detractors and had been described in a book attributed to Davy Crockett as a " . . . strut and swagger like a crow in the gutter." This was the eighth president of the United States, Martin Van Buren. A Democrat carrying forward Jacksonian policy, he told the Congress that day of the progress in the removal of the Cherokee Indians: "It affords me sincere pleasure to apprise the Congress of the entire removal of the Cherokee Nation of Indians to their new homes west of the Mississippi. The measures authorized by Congress at its last session have had the happiest effect . . . (The Cherokees) have migrated without apparent reluctance." The contradictory use of the words "removal" and "migrated" in the same paragraph pointed out the fraudulence of the entire affair. Most congressmen, friend or foe of the Cherokees, knew that the President's description of the enforced emigration of the entire Cherokee nation was a cynical falsehood.

On that same day, a traveler from Maine, passing through western Kentucky, encountered one of the thirteen detachments of Cherokees heading west. He later wrote in the *New York Observer:*

"On Tuesday we fell in with a detachment of the poor Cherokee indians . . . about 1,100 of them with 60 wagons, 600 horses, and perhaps 40 pairs of oxen. We found them in the forest camped for the night by the side of the road under a severe fall of rain, accompanied by heavy wind. With their canvas for a shield from the inclemency of the weather, and the cold, wet ground for a resting place, after the fatigue of the day, they spent the night. . . . We learned from the inhabitants on the road where the indians passed that they buried 14 or 15 at every stopping place, and they made a journey of ten miles per day only on the average . . . When I read in the President's message that he was happy to inform the Senate that the Cherokees were peaceably and without reluctance removed, and remembered that it was on the third day of December when not one of the detachments had reached their destination; and that a large majority had not even made half their journey when he made the declaration, I thought I wished the President could have been there that very day in Kentucky with myself, and have seen the comfort and willingness with which the Cherokees were making their journey."

Physically expelled by United States soldiers from their native lands—lands that had been secured to them by an endless series of treaties made with the immigrants from Europe—seventeen thousand men,

Sequoyah and the Cherokee alphabet which he developed

women, and children had been forced to leave behind their lands, homes, and possessions and make an eight-hundred-mile trek to a strange territory, there to try to rebuild their nation.

They had migrated once before during their remembered history. Of Iroquoian stock, they had fallen to warring with the rest of the Iroquois and had finally left their homelands around Lake Erie and drifted south into the mountain retreats of the southern Appalachians. From this lush, primeval land they carved out a new country for themselves consisting originally of present-day Kentucky and Tennessee and parts of West Virginia, Virginia, North and South Carolina, Georgia, Alabama, and Mississippi.

DeSoto's Spanish conquistadores, exploring that land in 1440, were the first Europeans to make contact with the tribe. They called them the Chalaque—their translation of the Indian name Tsalagi (the French adapted this to Cheraqui and the British to Cherokee). These first European intruders described the tribe as living ". . . on roots and herbs which they seek in the open field and on game killed with their arrows. The people are very domestic, go quite naked, and are very meek."

Within three hundred years of this first encounter, the Cherokees had developed a high degree of Old World sophistication, as attested to in an official United States government report of 1825 which said of the tribe: "The natives carry on considerable trade with adjoining states; (they) export cotton down the Mississippi . . . cultivate gardens and orchards. . . . Many public roads and houses of entertainment are kept by the natives . . . (There are) numerous and flourishing villages. . . . Cotton and woolen clothes are manufactured. A new town in the center of the nation . . . is the seat of government."

The report understated the extent of their civilization. The Cherokees had a written language in which

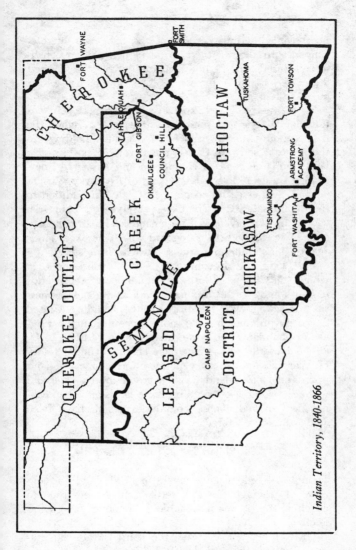

Indian Territory, 1840-1866

The division of the Indian Territory

nearly one hundred percent of the tribe was literate. This in turn allowed them to develop a written constitution—based upon the Constitution of the United States—a judicial system, schools, a newspaper, and a postal system.

Such "progress" was expensive: it cost the Cherokees their lands. The first such loss came in 1721 when the tribe ceded some of their South Carolina holdings to the white colony at Charleston. In 1775, an English land company, Richard Henderson and Associates, persuaded the tribe to sell large parts of Kentucky, Virginia, and Tennessee for a mere £10,000. In addition to these land sales, the Cherokee preserve was being devoured by the ravenous frontiersmen. The British government promised to safeguard the Cherokee lands against these white migrations, but with little effect.

Following the Revolutionary War (subsequent to which the Cherokees lost the remainder of their lands in South and North Carolina as well as most of Tennessee for siding with the British), the fledgling United States government had no more success than the English at containing the western settlers, as testified to by an official letter to the Cherokee chiefs: "The Secretary of War has spoken to you my mind about the land upon the Cumberland. . . . More than ten thousand (white) people are seated on these lands and they cannot be removed. These boundaries which have been made cannot be altered. . . .

G. Washington
Philadelphia, June 14th, 1794"

Though the federal government in 1794 could not conceive of "removing" white settlers, they were soon to conclude that it was reasonable to "remove" far greater numbers of Indians.

On October 2nd of 1798, the United States government signed the Treaty of Tellico with thirty-nine

Cherokee chiefs. The Treaty solemnly bound the United States to ". . . continue the guaranty of their (Cherokee) country forever." At the time of the Treaty of Tellico, the Cherokees had forty-three thousand square miles of land. By 1819, it had been reduced to fifteen thousand square miles. In addition the United States had forced the tribe to grant unrestricted road privileges through Cherokee lands, making that country all the more accessible to white settlers.

In 1802, the State of Georgia ceded to the United States her unoccupied western lands comprising the present-day states of Alabama and Mississippi. This "Georgia Compact of 1802" also provided that as part of the consideration for this land cession, the United States should, at its own expense, remove all Indians from Georgia ". . . as soon as it could be done peacefully and upon favorable terms." When President Thomas Jefferson made the Louisiana Purchase in 1803, he promptly suggested moving all of the eastern Indian tribes into that territory. Pursuant to that suggestion, Congress quickly passed an appropriations bill to expedite Jefferson's solution to the "Indian problem."

Some Cherokees, anticipating the loss of their homelands, had already started migrating westward as early as the middle 1700's. This exodus continued until, by 1815, there were nearly three thousand Cherokees living in what was to become the State of Arkansas.

In 1817, over the angry protests of the greater part of the Cherokee tribe, a body of Cherokees gave up their eastern lands to the United States in return for a permanent land grant in Arkansas. With the departure westward of these Cherokees, the Indian nation was divided into the western Cherokees, numbering about seven thousand, and the eastern Cherokees, who were more than twice as numerous and continued to reside in Georgia-Alabama-Tennessee.

Andrew Jackson at the Battle of New Orleans where he

gained national fame—with the help of his Indian allies

It was not many years, however, until the western Cherokees discovered that they had not gone far enough if they expected to escape the rapacity of the land-hungry whites. Some whites had already settled upon the Arkansas lands granted the Cherokees. These refused to leave, and if they were removed, quickly returned bringing others with them. Accordingly, yet another treaty was signed with the western Cherokees in 1828 by which the Indians agreed to give up their lands in Arkansas in exchange for a new grant of seven million acres in what is now Oklahoma.

At the same time, the eastern Cherokees were engaged in a struggle to save their nation from obliteration. Georgia was insistent that the Compact of 1802 be kept and all Indians removed from her territory, but the United States protested that the Indians were unwilling to go and nothing in the compact compelled the government to remove them against their will.

The federal government was, nonetheless, bringing all its powers of persuasion to bear against the Cherokees. The official attitude was succinctly expressed in 1824 by the vigorous Secretary of War, John C. Calhoun, when he told a group of Cherokee leaders: ". . . a distinct society or nation within the limits of a State is incompatible with our system."

On December 20, 1828, the State Legislature of Georgia extended state law over the Cherokees and their nation, the action to become effective June 1, 1830. This move was prompted in part by the lack of action by the federal government to remove the Cherokees. Far more instrumental in that legislative decision was the discovery of gold on the Indians' land earlier that same year; one of the laws the Georgians imposed upon the Cherokees was a ban against Indians mining gold on their own property.

In the bilingual Cherokee newspaper, the *Phoenix*,

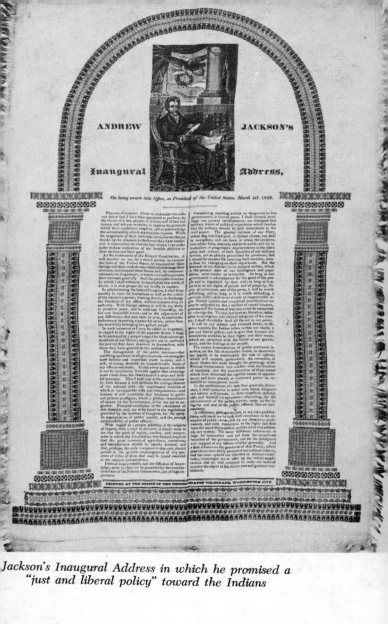

Jackson's Inaugural Address in which he promised a "just and liberal policy" toward the Indians

the editor, Elias Boudinot wrote of the situation: "The State of Georgia has taken a strong stand against us, and the U.S. must either defend us and our rights or leave us to our foe. In the latter case, she will violate her promise of protection, utterly disregarding her plighted faith, deprive us of the right of self-government and wrest from us our land. Then, in the deep anguish of our misfortunes, we may justly say there is no place of security for us, either here or beyond the Mississippi, and no confidence left that the U.S. will be more just and faithful toward us in the barren prairies of the west then here on the soil inherited from the Great Author of our existence."

The Cherokees had little reason to expect help from the federal government since the election in 1828 of Andrew Jackson. It was, in part, because of Jackson's election that the Georgia Legislature felt emboldened to extend jurisdiction over the Cherokee nation.

The year of Andrew Jackson's election to the Presidency also saw the election of a new chief of the Cherokees; both were men of inflexible will and determination preparing for a final showdown.

Andrew Jackson, the seventh president of the United States, had been elected as a Democrat. He was a colorful and popular figure. Tall, militarily erect, with his shock of thick white hair and his stern expression, he was a commanding leader. Disliked and distrusted by the educated Whigs of the eastern cities, Jackson drew most of his support from the West; this was Jackson the frontiersman and Indian fighter, a hero for the average man.

In the same year, 1828, the Cherokees elected a new chief: Guwisguwi, also known by the English name of John Ross. Of Cherokee and Scotch blood, Ross was a darkly handsome young man who was as comfortable in buckskins as ruffled shirts. The operator of a river ferry and the owner of a store, Ross had been a political leader in the tribe since 1819 when, at the age of twenty-nine, he was elected the first president of the National Council, the Cherokee equivalent of the U.S. Senate. He served in that post for eight years until he was elected principal chief of the Cherokees, an office he was to continue in for forty years.

Jackson and Ross were no strangers; they had fought together against a warring group of Creek Indians who had carried out a grisly massacre at Fort Simmons, in what is now Alabama. Many Cherokee leaders knew Andrew Jackson from that campaign against the "red stick" Creeks. In the Battle of Horseshoe Bend in 1814, Jackson promoted one Cherokee to the rank of major for his valour (he used the rank as a name and was known thereafter as Major Ridge), while, in the same battle, General Jackson's very life was saved by the Cherokee chief Junaluska.

Delegations of cultured erudite Cherokee representatives hastened to Washington to see the Chief Executive and present the tribal case. In some quarters of the Capitol, the Cherokees were still being vilified as "savages," though most Whigs in Washington wondered aloud if the real savages weren't the dirty, whisky-drinking backwoodsmen whom the president often entertained.

Any hopes the Cherokee delegates had of reviving their old comradeship with Andrew Jackson were quickly dashed. The removal of the Indians was politically expedient to Jackson whose backing came from western settlers. He considered any means proper in order to be rid of the Indians, and later when the Cherokees proved to be tenacious, Jackson showed the extent of his disregard for them when he snapped: "I favor leaving the poor, deluded Cherokees to their fate and their annihilation."

In 1830, the United States Congress passed a bill for the removal of the Indians. It did not allow for forceful removal, but provided President Jackson with power and money to negotiate treaties with the tribes in order to remove them to the West. This Removal Bill passed by only a slight margin, proof that the Cherokees were not without allies. In fact, their friends were numerous and prestigious, including such powerful men as Henry Clay, Noah Webster, and John Adams. Even amongst the frontiersmen the Cherokees were well represented; Davy Crockett spoke for them in the Senate, and Sam Houston, an adopted Cherokee himself, pleaded the Cherokee case before Andrew Jackson.

But the Cherokee's situation continued to deteriorate. Several days after the passage of the Removal Bill, Georgia extended sovereignty over the part of the Cherokee nation that occupied that state. The Cherokee government was hindered in its operation, Cherokees were arrested by the Georgia militia on the slightest provocation, whites accused of crimes in Cherokee lands were removed from the jurisdiction of Indian courts and usually freed by white juries, and a period of general harassment of the Cherokees began under the sanction of Georgia law.

Chief John Ross brought suit in the courts to establish Cherokee property rights. His case, "The Cherokees vs. Georgia," brought before the Supreme Court in January, 1831, was dismissed on the grounds that the Cherokees were a ". . . domestic dependent nation" with the United States as guardian, and therefore the tribe could not maintain the action in the courts.

There followed a second court case brought against the State of Georgia by the Reverend Samuel Worcester, a Vermont missionary indicted by the State of Georgia for continuing his residence in the Cherokee nation without taking an oath of allegiance to Georgia. His suit, "Worchester vs. Georgia," was appealed in March, 1832, to the United States Supreme Court,

John Ross led the bitter Cherokee fight against removal to the Indian Territory.

which handed down a decision in Worcester's favor declaring the Georgia law relating to the Indians unconstitutional and the law in his indictment null and void. When President Jackson heard of this decision favorable to the Cherokees, he angrily announced: "John Marshall (Chief Justice of the Supreme Court) has made his decision; let him enforce it now if he can!"

John Ridge, a Cherokee spokesman in Washington at the time, wrote to a friend in the Cherokee nation: ". . . the contest is not over . . . time is to settle the matter either for us and all the friends of the Judiciary, or against us all." In that same letter, he spoke about a government report which falsely declared that most Cherokees were in favor of removal, then went on to conclude: "(If) the government succeeded in making a treaty with a fraction or faction of our nation . . . it would never be ratified by the Senate constituted as it was, as we assuredly would protest against it and defeat it."

It was to be one of the sad ironies of the Cherokee removal that John Ridge was to be one of the leaders of that faction that eventually did sign the Treaty for Removal.

Georgia continued its harassment of the Cherokees, declaring martial law in the Cherokee nation. All Cherokee assemblies were disbanded, and the Indian government continued only by conducting business in the Alabama section of the nation.

At the same time, the federal government continued to bring pressure on the Cherokees to remove. Among other ploys, secret government agents attempted to bribe various of the chiefs to sign a removal treaty.

Some of the Cherokee leaders began to lose their resolve as they realized that the whites surrounding their nation were implacable, and as their missions to Washington continued to bear no fruit. Their despondence was summed up by John Ridge who wrote from

Washington on March 10, 1835: "[Chief John] Ross has failed before the Senate, before the Secretary of War, and before the President."

It was in this mood of defeat that five hundred Cherokees, led by Major Ridge, his son John, Elias Boudinot, Stand Waite and a number of other prominent Cherokees, met with a U.S. commissioner to sign a treaty ceding to the United States the last of the Cherokee lands in the East. The treaty was concluded on December 29, 1835.

The Cherokees were bitter and angry over the unrepresentative treaty; those who were a party to it were accused of treason and threatened with the "blood law"—a law which demanded death for any Cherokee ceding tribal lands against the will of the tribe. One of the treaty men, Major Ridge, had assassinated another Cherokee, Doublehead, in 1802 for breaking the same blood law. [On the night of June 22, 1839, in the new Cherokee territory—now Oklahoma—three of the treaty men, Major Ridge, John Ridge, and Elias Boudinot, were murdered for having signed the treaty.]

John Ross refused to recognize the treaty, proclaiming: "It cannot bind us because we did not make it. It was made by a few unauthorized individuals and the Nation is not a party in it."

When the treaty was submitted to the United States Senate for ratification, it passed by a majority of a single vote after a close and bitter fight.

Chief Ross circulated a petition among the tribe repudiating the treaty and declaring it unrepresentative. Of a Cherokee population of seventeen thousand, nearly sixteen thousand people signed the petition. It was ignored.

Brevet Brigadier General John E. Wool was sent to the Cherokee nation to make sure the Cherokees started no trouble. He found, instead, that the only trouble was caused by the suppressive whites, and Wool quickly came to sympathize with the Indians. His attempts to protect the Cherokees in Alabama led to that state's charge that the general was disturbing the peace, a charge which Wool was quickly cleared of by a military court of inquiry.

General Wool reported to the Secretary of War: ". . . the Cherokees to a man oppose the treaty . . . The scene since I have been in this country has been nothing but a heart-rending one . . . If I could—and I could not do them a greater kindness—I would remove every Indian tomorrow beyond the reach of the white man, who, like vultures, are watching, ready to pounce upon their prey and strip them of everything they have . . ." Finally, Wool asked to be relieved of his command on moral grounds.

With the election of Martin Van Buren to the Presidency of the United States, the last hope of the Cherokees was brought to a bitter end. Van Buren was a Democrat; he was Jackson's man. He echoed Jacksonian policy when he said: "No State can achieve proper culture, civilization, and progress in safety as long as Indians are permitted to remain."

This, in spite of the fact that the highly civilized Cherokee nation was about to be overrun by an illiterate white rabble.

The entire Cherokee nation was to remove west within two years after the Congress had ratified the treaty. By the time that deadline arrived, May 26, 1838, only two thousand Cherokees had left their homelands and so the United States government resorted to force: Major General Winfield S. Scott, with four thousand soldiers of the 4th Artillery, 4th Infantry, and 3rd Dragoons plus three thousand volunteer troops entered the Cherokee nation to physically carry out the removal:

"Cherokees, the President of the United States has

sent me with a powerful army to cause you, in obedience to the Treaty of 1835, to join that part of your people who are already established in prosperity on the other side of the Mississippi. Unhappily, the two years which were allowed for the purpose, you have suffered to pass away without following. . . . By the time this solemn address shall reach your distant settlements, the emigration must be commenced in haste . . . The full moon of May is already on the wane, and before another shall have passed away, every Cherokee man, woman, and child . . . must be in motion to join their brethren in the west. . . . Thousands and thousands (of my troops) are approaching from every quarter, to tender resistance and escape hopeless . . . Will you then, by resistance, compel us to resort to arms? . . . I am an old warrior, and have been present at many a scene of slaughter; but spare me, I beseech you, the horror of witnessing the destruction of the Cherokees."

That the removal was as free of violence as it was, is a credit first of all to John Ross, who forbade his people to forcefully resist the soldiers. Many Cherokees were prepared to defend their homes and lands to the death, but Ross was determined that the removal should not become a bloodbath. His ally in this goal was Winfield Scott, who was not unsympathetic to the Cherokees' plight and, as best he could, restrained his soldiers from using violent force.

It was incredible that during the initial removal, only one violent death occurred. A soldier was killed by a Cherokee man, Tsali, who became violently angry when the soldier prodded Tsali's wife in the back with a bare bayonet. Tsali and his sons escaped to the hills where over a thousand Cherokees had already fled to escape the soldiers. General Scott decided to make an example of Tsali in order to discourage any more attacks against his soldiers. He asked that Tsali give himself up, promising in return to allow those Cherokees

An artist's sketch depicting the Cherokee mode of dress at the time of their removal to Oklahoma

hiding in the hills to remain there. Tsali surrendered himself and was publicly executed.

Thirteen stockade forts had been constructed along the Tennessee River and at other key centers in the Indian lands to be used as collection points and detention areas for the Cherokees until they could be sent west.

The seven thousand soldiers under Scott's command had spread throughout the Cherokee nation to drive the Indians to these stockades. Squads of armed and mounted soldiers swooped down upon cabins, homes, and plantations, surprising the Cherokee inhabitants and taking them prisoner. The captives were marched off as quickly as possible to the nearest concentration camp.

Following the soldiers was a jubilant white rabble who looted the Indian homes as soon as the owners had been prodded away at bayonet point. Houses were ransacked and burned, crops destroyed, livestock driven off, and graves plundered. The State of Georgia attempted to maintain order by holding a lottery to distribute the land taken from the Cherokees.

In the first hot, dry week of June, a group of eight hundred Cherokees were put aboard a conglomeration of riverboats that were to carry them up the Tennessee River to the Ohio River, then down the Mississippi and finally to the Arkansas River. The next week, Lieutenant Robert Whiteley took a second group of 875 Cherokees aboard flatboats up the Tennessee. Three more parties set out along the river route. When news returned of the soaring death rate amongst the Cherokees en route, Chief Ross anxiously pleaded with General Scott to allow the Cherokees to superintend their own removal.

Scott agreed, happy to be rid of the onerous job, though Scott's decision was to raise the ire of Jackson and other Democrat leaders. On July 25, Scott and Ross reached an agreement by which the Cherokees

Elias Boudinot

would be responsible for their own removal provided all detachments were on their way no later than the last of October.

In the short time allotted them, the Cherokees arranged with private white contractors to transport the remaining thirteen thousand Cherokees across an eight hundred mile overland route. It was to be a tremendous undertaking requiring 645 wagons and teams, tons of foodstuffs, guides, interpreters, and teamsters. The cost was computed at $66 per person for the eight hundred mile trip, or $66,000 for each of the thirteen detachments. White contractors swarmed to the Cherokee nation, prepared to make a handsome profit from the Indians' plight.

The first detachment, undersigned, with only 850 people, left in the middle of September under the direction of Elijah Hicks. The route they took led northwest to Nashville, Tennessee, into western Kentucky across the lower tip of Illinois, through the southeastern corner of Missouri, and then across Arkansas to Fort Gibson in the Indian territories. Each following detachment took the same approximate route, altering it in order to find game along the way.

It was estimated by the contractors that, at the longest, the journey could take no more than eighty days. In no case did any detachment reach its destination in less than four months, and for many, it was to last as long as a half-year.

No sooner had the first detachment left than trouble set in. Unseasonably heavy rains drenched the route, turning the primitive roads and trails into morasses of mud and water. Wagons often mired axle or bed deep in the muck churned up by the passage of the large number of wagons and people. The march progressed slowly as the weary Cherokees were repeatedly put to the task of manually dragging the mired wagons free.

Beyond the Mississippi River, the condition of the

Chief Major Ridge

roads was atrocious. In fact, except for one military road through southeastern Missouri to Little Rock and Fort Smith, there really were only trails. In many lays. To try to hurry the march, the profit-hungry consisting of a trail along which the trees had been razed to the ground, presenting a special hazard for the teamsters. If the roads were difficult, the wet bottomed prairies, the river bogs, and the hill trails were pure hell.

Another problem faced by the Cherokees was the river crossings. The system of ferries along the line of march was not good under any circumstances; with the rivers swollen by flood waters and choked with the ice of early winter, river crossings usually meant long delays. To try to hurry the march, the profit-hungry contractors often overloaded the rickety and inadequate river ferries. On one crossing of the Mississippi, a ferry carrying twice its fifty person capacity sank in mid-river; only a few were saved.

Still, there was no alternative for the Cherokees, and the detachments continued to set out. Behind Elijah Hicks came Hair Conrad leading a party of 850. Surely none of them realized that before they reached their new homeland four months later over two hundred of them would die. The third detachment to set out was led by Jesse Bushyhead and consisted of a thousand persons. By mid-October, the Reverend Evan Jones departed with his contingent of 1,250 Cherokees. To compensate for some of the small detachments, some of the later groups consisted of up to two thousand people.

The early winter was a killing enemy to these travelers who, in most cases, had been provided with only a single blanket. In addition to the cold, there was malnutrition. Their diets often consisted of salt pork and corn, with coffee sweetened with molasses. The contractors, who had planned to buy food along the route, often found prices inflated and so bought less than

*A detail from Robert Lindneux's dramatic
version of the trail of tears*

needed in order to try and conserve profits. The weakness of malnutrition in turn made the Cherokees easy victims of diseases such as cholera and smallpox.

Each Cherokee campsite was scarred with the mounded earth of new graves. Besides the dead, the seriously ill or dying were left behind with friends or relatives; they could not keep up with the march, and the march could not stop. Few of those that dropped out ever rejoined their party. Many times the stragglers became the prey of wild animals. One Cherokee woman and her two small children were found along an Arkansas roadside mauled to death—most likely by mountain lions. As vicious as the animals were the desperados who waylaid travelers, often murdering the victim they robbed or raped. The Missouri border was especially infested with these desperados who lived in abandoned cabins or in caves near the roads.

The Cherokees' only protection was in staying with their contingent. These trains of wagons and marchers could often stretch for ten miles back along the route of travel. Some required an entire day to pass a town.

There were many white communities through which they passed on their way west. In some they were treated well, given water, food, and what comfort the overwhelmed citizens could offer. In Jacksonville, Illinois, the city band even gave a concert for the Cherokees at their evening encampment outside the city. But for the most part, townspeople turned out to gawk and jeer at the weary Indians. Tradesmen made profit by selling food, blankets, and other necessities to the Cherokees at triple and quadruple prices. And many unscrupulous whites were happy to sell whiskey to the disheartened Indians.

In most towns along the line of march, the citizenry was warned well in advance of the approach of the Cherokees. Townspeople would hurry to hide anything of value for fear the Cherokees would steal anything they could! Some cities refused to let the Indians pass through, but required them to detour, fearing thefts, disorder, or disease. Little Rock, Arkansas, afraid of contamination from some of the contingents, made them travel south of the city, forcing them to endure the Fourche Bayou, a wild, malarial swamp.

With each delay, the white contractors saw their profits slipping away. The only balancing factor in their favor was that each Cherokee who died along the way represented a savings. There were many such savings for the contractors. Out of nearly seventeen thousand Cherokees who started the westward march, four thousand died. When the last contingent of Cherokees arrived in the Indian Territory on March 26, 1839, and the tally of dead and missing had been taken, not one family in the tribe had escaped without loss.

James Mooney, in his account of the Cherokee removal drawn from interviews with survivors of the march —both Cherokees and white officers—quotes a Georgia volunteer, afterward a colonel in the Confederate Army, as saying: "I fought through the Civil War and have seen men shot to pieces and slaughtered by the thousands, but the Cherokee Removal was the cruelest work I ever knew."

Little wonder that this removal march of the Cherokee nation has come to be known as "The Trail of Tears."

Custer's last charge at the Little Big Horn

THE EPIC FLIGHT OF THE CHEYENNES

by Norman B. Wiltsey

*A*fter defeating Colonel Custer and his Seventh Cavalry at the Little Big Horn on June 25, 1876, the allied Plains tribes scattered in all directions. No feasting and dancing followed this greatest of all Indian victories over the soldiers, so fearful were the chiefs of the Great White Father's vengeance for the deaths of Custer and 226 of his troopers.

Within a few days of the Custer battle—erroneously branded a "foul massacre" by the inflamed Eastern press—the aroused army was gathering to march again, and this time in irresistible force. Sitting Bull led part of the Sioux on a leisurely journey to a temporary refuge in Canada; Crazy Horse and his Oglalas "stayed out" until May of 1877 when the young leader sadly decided to surrender at Camp Robinson, where he was murdered by a white soldier in September of that year.

The Cheyenne chiefs Dull Knife and Little Wolf, heading a band of two hundred lodges with about four hundred, moved on to the Bighorn Mountains after the climactic battle and went into camp near the head of Powder River. Dull Knife was weary and depressed; he announced at council that no member of his band would henceforth pull a trigger in battle unless first attacked. His statement was received in silence by his subchiefs. Only Black Hairy Dog, Keeper of the Sacred Medicine Arrows, agreed with the chief that their only chance of survival lay in making peace with the whites.

Late in November, 1876, with the Eastern newspapers still clamoring for revenge for Custer's death, General Mackenzie's cavalry moved out of Fort Fetterman with general instructions from C.O. General Crook to "round up or destroy all hostiles encountered." Mackenzie was actually hunting Crazy Horse's elusive band of Oglala Sioux, but his scouts brought word of Dull Knife's village on the Powder and the general altered his plans in accordance.

Against Dull Knife's four hundred warriors, Mackenzie could throw eight hundred men, nearly half of whom were Indians recruited from reservations. Indicative of the confused and tragic times was the fact that a number of Mackenzie's 363 Indians were Cheyennes.

Dull Knife's camp lay in a deep craterlike valley in a fold of the Bighorns. Narrow passes slashed the high, rocky walls of the valley, which was centrally traversed by a shallow stream lined with cottonwoods and heavy brush. The Cheyenne lodges were grouped along this stream in the center of the valley.

Bitter dissension wracked the Cheyenne camp on the evening of November 25. Scouts had discovered the approaching troops while they were yet forty miles away, and Dull Knife thought it best to strike the lodges at once and flee deeper into the mountains. Young Two Moons (nephew of Chief Two Moons) warned that many Indians, including the hated Pawnees, accompanied the white troops and that a "big fight" was certain if they remained encamped in the valley. Black Hairy Dog urged that everybody move out at once.

Last Bull, chief of the powerful Fox Soldier Society, disagreed violently with Dull Knife and Black Hairy Dog. He made a fiery speech to the assembled warriors, inquiring sarcastically if they were men or old women. As for himself, the Fox Soldier chief declared fiercely, *he* would stay and fight the soldiers and their renegade Indian friends all by himself if others turned coward and ran off into the mountains. Little Wolf, war chief of the band, electrified the meeting and brought the wavering braves neatly into line by leaping to his feet with a whoop and proposing an immediate scalp dance. The clever ploy decided the issue instantaneously.

The temperature stood at well below zero in the snow-covered valley, but that made no difference to the excited Cheyennes. All night long, the warriors danced and sang around the blazing fires to the savage rhythm of drum and flute and rattle. Near dawn, just as the mad dance was ending and the tired participants made ready for bed, the Pawnee of Mackenzie's command crept close to the unaccountably unguarded camp, lining up the attack.

Dawn was breaking when the general gave the order to charge the village. His Indian scouts had been placed carefully around the camp, with Major North's Pawnees leading the assault on the right. Just behind the Pawnees rode the cavalry, with instructions to surround the lodges and prevent the Cheyennes' escape.

The attack was perfectly timed and smartly executed. Almost all of the warriors had left the dance by this time and were sleeping naked in their lodges. North's shrieking Pawnees swept straight through the village to

115

Battle of the Little Big Horn, June 25, 1876

Custer's last rally at the Little Big Horn

General Custer's death struggle

the stream in the middle. Here their horses bogged down in the half-frozen mud, giving the Cheyennes along the opposite bank precious time to hustle the women and children off into the maze of gulches and ravines beyond their lodges. That accomplished, the warriors seized their guns and took up a position in a deep gully from which they could fire into the invaders from cover.

Mackenzie quickly spotted this maneuver of the Cheyennes and ordered Lieutenant McKinney, with Company M of the Fourth Cavalry, to dislodge them. The warriors waited coolly until the troopers were almost upon them before firing. McKinney went down, riddled by six bullets. Four men in line beside him were knocked off their horses by the terrific blast of rifle fire, and the attack piled up in disorder. The Cheyennes whooped in triumph and dashed from cover to count coup on the fallen troopers, thereby exposing themselves to a deadly counterattack.

Captain Hamilton, leading a supporting company of the Fifth Cavalry, now charged the Cheyennes and wiped them out almost to a man. Hamilton himself killed two braves with his saber. Thirty warriors died in furious hand-to-hand fighting before the few survivors broke away and fled into the rocky slopes back of the camp.

The fight now resolved into a long-range sniping match between the opposing forces. Psychology was tried on both sides. Cheyenne-speaking scout Bill Rowland called out to the Cheyennes to surrender, and the Cheyennes shouted back defiantly. Dull Knife, alone, mourning that he had lost three sons in the fighting, said he was ready to make peace. The aging chief also took this opportunity to thank the soldier-chief for not killing women and children. He was repeating his offer to surrender when Little Wolf broke in angrily to denounce Mackenzie's Indian scouts. "Go home, you have no business here!" shouted Little Wolf. "We can whip these white men alone, but we can't fight Indians, too. You men ought to be ashamed of yourselves. *Go home!*"

By noon the fight had slipped away into the hills, heading for Crazy Horse's Oglala camp on distant Beaver Creek. They had only a few horses, a dozen buffalo robes and little clothing. Behind them, the Pawnees and the cavalry promptly set to work firing the camp. Everything was destroyed in that roaring holocaust: robes, blankets, saddles, kettles, hides, and clothing. The buffalo and antelope meat so painstakingly collected to feed the band through the winter months was burned, along with fat, marrow, and tallow preserved in scores of buffalo bladders. Seven hundred ponies had been captured; one hundred of these the thrifty Pawnees were allowed to load with weapons and choice plunder and keep for themselves.

Eleven children froze to death during the Cheyennes' desperate flight through the storm-swept mountains to the camp of Crazy Horse. All the horses had to be killed for food before the terrible journey was ended. Old women saved their lives by thrusting hands and feet into warm entrails of the butchered horses; old men, unable to walk further, lay down quietly in the drifting snow to wait for death. Warriors, raging silently against the white destroyers and their treacherous Indian allies, vowed vengeance in full measure once they had joined forces with Crazy Horse and his Oglalas.

Crazy Horse disappointed them. The great young fighting leader of the Sioux flatly refused to join the Cheyennes in reckless last-ditch reprisals against the whites. Gladly, he supplied them with horses, robes, and clothing, and shared his scanty food supply—but he would not agree to fight the whites again. "It is useless," said Crazy Horse with fatalistic calm. "Twice we have defeated them, at the Rosebud and again at the Greasy Grass (Little Bighorn), and still they march against us in greater strength than ever. The *Wasicus* outnumber the blades of grass on the prairie; we Indians can no longer stand against them. Friend *Shahielas*, it is time for all to be smart and prepare to walk the white man's road. Otherwise we shall *all* be killed!"

Dull Knife agreed with Crazy Horse. "What you say is true, my son. We Cheyennes are through trying to fight the whirlwind. We will surrender to the white soldier-chiefs and try to live as white men do."

The Cheyennes surrendered to General Nelson Miles at Fort Keogh in the spring of 1877. Thirty young braves, still seething at Crazy Horse's "betrayal," promptly enlisted as scouts with Miles' cavalry to assist in rounding up the Sioux. The remainder of the band was sent south to Darlington Reservation, Indian Territory (now Oklahoma), to live with their relatives—the Southern Cheyennes.

At first it seemed that the peace and prosperity so ardently desired for his people by Dull Knife was now to be their lot. Gradually, however, the chief came bitterly to realize that he had been duped by the smoother-talking white men into consenting to a fatal move. The whites had lied when they said there was plenty of game on the reservation. The buffalo had long been exterminated there, and five thousand Arapahoes and Southern Cheyennes had made short work of killing off the smaller game. Too proud to beg from their relatives or the Arapahoes, the newly arrived Northern Cheyennes began to starve. Fever decimated them; within a year of their arrival from the dry and healthful climate of Montana and North Dakota, more than half of them were dead.

Agent John Miles testified before a Senate committee that he never received supplies to provide for the Indians for more than nine months of each fiscal year. The

Chief Two Moons, leader of the Cheyennes
at Little Big Horn

Indians were lifelong meat eaters, and what few beeves the government furnished them were little more than skin and bone. It was inevitable that they should soon sicken and die. The single physician stationed at the agency, who had more than five thousand Indians in his care, was not provided with medicines by the Indian Bureau for months on end. Medical supplies, which that year should have been available in the summer, were not received until the following January.

About the middle of August, 1878, Dull Knife and Little Wolf went to plead with Agent Miles to allow the Cheyennes to go home. Dull Knife was too ill and shaky to talk; Little Wolf acted as his spokesman. Edmond Guerrier acted as interpreter for the two Cheyenne chiefs.

The war chief talked slowly and with grave earnestness in Miles's office, facing the agent and two army officers from nearby Fort Reno: "We have come to ask the agent that we be sent home to our own country in the mountains. My people were raised there, in a land of pines and clear, cold rivers. There, we were always healthy, for there was meat enough for all. We were happy there until the Great Father's soldiers brought us here. Now, in the year that we have been in this southern country, many of us have died. This is not a good place for us—there is too much heat and dust and not enough food. We wish to return to our home in the mountains. If you have not the power to give us permission to go back there, let some of us go on to Washington and tell them there how it is; or do you write to Washington and get permission for us to go back North?"

Agent Miles, harassed by a hundred exasperating problems, wearily answered, "That is a fine speech, Little Wolf, but I cannot do what you ask. Stay here for one more year and then I will see what can be done for you."

Little Wolf shook his head. "No, we cannot stay here another year; we want to go now. Before another year has passed, we may be all dead and there will be none of us *left* to travel North. *We must go now!*"

Miles had spoken the truth: He could do nothing. Seeming to realize this, the two chiefs accepted a gift of tobacco and left the agent's office. Through the window, Miles watched the gaunt Cheyennes riding their skinny ponies down the trail that led to their desolate camp. A hot, dry wind whipped dust into the faces of the Indians, and the agent could hear their hollow coughing as they rode hunched against the earthern storm.

Miles cursed fervently and returned to his desk. For a moment he considered writing yet another letter to Washington describing the pitiful plight of mountain-bred Indians exiled to the southern hell-hole of blazing sun, endlessly blowing red dust and no game. Then he shrugged hopelessly and cast the foolish thought aside. Useless—and too damn hot to write anyway.

Three weeks after his first confrontation with Agent Miles, Little Wolf was peremptorily summoned to the agent's office. Miles was upset and angry over a report by one of his Indian police officers that three young braves of Little Wolf's band had run away from the reservation. He demanded the the Cheyenne war chief turn over ten of his young men as hostages until soldiers had caught the runaways.

Calmly Little Wolf replied: "I cannot do what you ask. If I gave you those ten men you would never set them free, for the soldiers will never find those who have run off. They will hide as the coyote hides by day, and ride at night until they reach their home in the mountains."

This firm statement coming from the tattered scarecrow before him was just the added irritation required to snap Miles's sadly frayed patience. "You must do as

Frederic Remington's The Last Stand *showing troops attacked by the Cheyennes*

I say!" snapped the agent. "Otherwise I shall give your people no rations. You shall starve until these men are given to me!"

Upon receiving the translation of this harsh statement, Little Wolf studied Miles's angry countenance for a moment, then glanced searchingly at the stern faces of two army officers who stood beside the agent, as at their previous meeting. What the chief observed in the faces of these three white men seemed to make up his mind at once. He looked Miles straight in the eyes and spoke slowly and precisely so that there could be no mistaking his words. "We have been hungry ever since we were brought to this country, so you cannot frighten us with loud talk of starving. Many nights the children have gone to sleep with nothing but grass in their swollen bellies. Will you take the *grass* from them?" Little Wolf paused courteously, waiting for the agent to reply.

Miles ignored the chief's question and repeated his demand for the ten hostages.

Little Wolf continued: "I am now going back to my camp. I do not wish the ground about this agency to be made bloody, but now listen to what I say to you. I am going to leave here; I am going north to my own country. If you are going to send soldiers after me, I wish that you would let me get a little distance away from this agency. Then if you want to fight, I will fight you and we can make the ground bloody at that place."

The chief ceremoniously shook hands with Miles and the two officers and left the agent's office. The three white men seemed oddly stunned by the Indian's determined words and made no move to detain him.

Next morning at daybreak the Cheyennes started out boldly for the Powder River country that was home, fifteen hundred miles away: Three hundred people, including about eighty warriors, under the leadership of Dull Knife and Little Wolf. Actually, since Dull Knife was more counsellor than fighter, the entire responsibility for the safety of the band fell upon the war chief.

Late in the afternoon of the second day of their flight, two companies of cavalry caught up with the runaways. The Cheyennes were camped on Little Medicine Lodge River just across the Kansas line, resting their weary ponies and cooking almost the last of their carefully hoarded food supply.

Captain Murray, the cavalry commander, sent an Arapahoe scout into the Cheyennes' camp to parley. Little Wolf came forward to meet him, after giving his warriors precise instructions: "Do not shoot until the troopers have fired. Let them shoot first. I will go out and talk to them. If they shoot, I will be the first man killed. Then you can fight."

Ghost Man, the Arapahoe scout, called out nervously to Little Wolf: "The white men want you to go back. If you surrender and return to the reservation, they will give you rations and treat you well."

Little Wolf answered carefully, so that he would not be misunderstood: "Tell them that we do not want to fight; that we will not go back. I have no quarrel with anyone. I hold up my right hand that I do not wish to fight with the whites; but we are going to our old home to stay there. I will go alone to your chief and tell him this myself, so there can be no mistake."

Ghost Man then went back toward the troops and Little Wolf, unarmed, followed after him to talk to his commander. A nervous soldier squeezed off a carbine at the approaching Cheyenne, and Little Wolf turned and waved his warriors to the attack. The Cheyennes charged and drove the cavalry back from their camp. Fighting continued sporadically until dark. Three soldiers were killed in this brush, including a sergeant and the Arapahoe scout. Five Cheyennes were wounded.

At dull dawn of a dismal rainy day, Murray had his dismounted troopers moving in thin skirmish line upon

*The meeting between Sitting Bull and
General Nelson A. Miles*

Frederic Remington

the Cheyenne lodges. The captain was hopeful of catching the tired Indians sleeping and capturing the lot of them without further bloodshed. Halfway up the sharp rise of ground where the Cheyennes had pitched their tepees, Murray stopped and stared in amazement. The "tired Indians" were awake and waiting for him—in *trenches!* During the night Little Wolf and his people had dug furiously in the wet earth, and now they were crouched behind leveled gunbarrels and drawn bows; entrenched and ready to repel the soldiers' expected charge.

The captain felt a sudden sharp jolt of dismay, followed instantly by a surge of unreasoning anger. What manner of men were these damned, stubborn savages who lacked the simple jackass sense to know that they couldn't whip the U.S. Army? He gave the command to attack and a wave of fire flashed along the front of the Cheyennes' trench. Mechanically, Murray distinguished the murderous hiss of arrows amid the familiar rattle of carbines, the spiteful crack of Colts and the heavy boom of a Sharps buffalo gun. Retreating down the hill behind his shattered skirmish line, the commander realized in grateful surprise that the Indians' fire had stopped immediately when the soldiers turned and ran.

Four more troopers dead, twenty wounded; Murray swore with heartfelt eloquence as he made the grim count. The C.O. cooled off by making the wounded as comfortable as possible in the tents. Then he dispatched a courier to Fort Dodge for reinforcements, a howitzer, a medical officer, and wagons to transport the dead and the more seriously wounded men back to the hospital. There would be no more reckless attempts to round up the Cheyennes. Murray set pickets to watch the runaways while he awaited the arrival of the howitzer from Dodge. A few shells dropped down their muddy red necks would soon induce them to surrender.

Despite all precautions, the Indians slipped away

during the night and resumed their flight to the north. Three days later, Captain Murray's grimly pursuing troopers, accompanied by an uninvited posse of civilians led by Sheriff Bat Masterson of Dodge City, blundered onto the fleeing Indians in a fold of the prairie. Disregarding Masterson's shouted command to let the soldiers open the battle, the whooping posse galloped wildly to the attack. The warriors fired a single smashing volley, then charged, yelling the blood-chilling Cheyenne scalp cry. The civilians broke and fled, hopelessly impeding the cavalry by their headlong flight. Ponies at a dead run, the Cheyennes streamed on toward the Arkansas River.

Before the fugitives reached the Arkansas the raging troopers, quirting their horses at every jump, overtook them. Again, the warriors stood off the soldiers in a vicious skirmish that lasted for hours. Stopped cold by the accurate fire of Cheyenne sharpshooters hidden in the tumbled hills along the river, the troopers brought up supply wagons and used them as cover. The badly needed howitzer had failed to catch up with the cavalry. Darkness ended the stubborn fighting, and the Indians escaped once more, elusive as wisps of smoke in the wind.

On the Arkansas, the hungry Cheyennes came upon a party of hide hunters and captured them without firing a shot. The six white men were so dumbfounded at the sight of the traveling Indian village that they never made a move to fight. The Cheyennes took their guns —six heavy Sharps rifles—and the eighteen buffaloes they had killed, and let them go unharmed. The women prepared a feast of sizzling buffalo ribs and fat hump meat, and the gaunt warriors ate well for the first time in more than a year. Even Dull Knife, somber and preoccupied with worry about the ominous future, became cheerful after the feast and sat before his lodge smiling and smoking his pipe while the children played.

The fugitives camped that night on a little creek and crossed the Arkansas the next day. Hunters shot buffaloes with the new rifles, while the women made breastworks on the low hills back of camp. Scouts posted on the highest hill reported soldiers following their trail on the morning of the second day of their stay in this camp. The Cheyennes retreated behind their breastworks and waited for the troops to make their move.

The soldiers corralled their wagons in plain sight of the watching Indians, then dismounted and marched toward the breastworks in scattered formation. Little Wolf sat in front of the fortifications, calmly smoking his battered corncob pipe and talking encouragingly to his warriors. "See how silly these white men fight! Already they are wasting ammunition shooting at us, though they are beyond good rifle range. Let them come on; do not fire a shot. Lie quiet; make sure your guns are loaded and ready."

A bullet kicked up dirt near Little Wolf, but the chief did not flinch. "Don't get excited," he told a jittery youngster near him. "Keep calm and listen to me." By this time the troopers had begun to climb the hill, and Little Wolf said: "Now fire and let every bullet count for a man!"

The Cheyennes began a steady fire, and the troops broke and fled in disorder, leaving half a dozen dead on the field. Their officers pulled them together and started them up the hill again, but they could not reach the top. Desultory firing continued until dark, when the soldiers retreated to their wagon corral. The Cheyennes moved out under cover of darkness and turned the heads of their ponies northward.

They went straight north for three days, keen-eyed Dog Soldiers guarding the flanks and rear of the hurrying cavalcade. Little Wolf rode tirelessly in the lead, keeping an eye on everything. Behind them, their lengthening trail was marked by the graves of six dead. Age-old tribal laws dictated that the bodies of braves killed in battle must be left lying on the prairie for wolves and coyotes to devour; but Little Wolf himself had ordered the burials and directed that the whole village should ride straight over each grave so that no vengeful white man should ever find and desecrate these lasting resting places of Cheyenne warriors.

A dozen wounded fighting men and nearly as many exhausted old people jounced along uncomplainingly in pony drags. Sometimes, incredibly, these helpless ones would muster strength to sing "Brave Heart" songs of encouragement to the warriors. All were merry, for they were going home.

Around the fleeing Indians the telegraph wires crackled messages to outlying army posts: "Watch for the Cheyennes!" Back in Washington, General-in-Chief of the Army, William Tecumseh Sherman, wrote an order placing General George Crook in overall command of the hunt for the impudent runaways who had outfought and outrun every military force that could be thrown against them. Crook, an experienced Indian fighter, increased the number of soldiers in the field until thirteen thousand were engaged in the search. A vast cordon of troops was thrown across Kansas and Nebraska with but a single mission; to trap less than three hundred Indians. Trains bearing howitzers and artillerymen patrolled the railroads; jumpy train crews peered anxiously across the rolling prairies, vainly trying to catch sight of the fugitives.

Near Ogalalla, on the South Platte, the Cheyennes slipped through the troops by bolding fording the stream at a point midway between two cavalry camps. On the north shore of the river they split into small parties, wrapped the hoofs of their ponies with strips

The Crazy Horse Fight, January 8, 1877,
by Frederic Remington

torn from their blankets, and passed silently as shadows within a hundred yards of the pickets. One sentinel reported hearing a "queer sound" about midnight but noticed nothing more. The sound was an Indian pony's snort of alarm choked off by strong fingers before it had hardly started.

Across the river and well past the cavalry camps, the Cheyennes reunited and pushed on to the North Platte. Here, near the mouth of White Clay Creek, they stopped for a full day to rest and attend to the wounded.

At White Clay Creek the band of hunted Indians split up. Content to be back in familiar territory and bone-weary of being chased like predatory animals, Dull Knife and about 150 followers decided to go into Red Cloud agency and surrender. The gentle, aging counselor was oddly certain that *this* time the Great Father in Washington would listen kindly to his plea and allow his people to remain for a time at the agency in peace. Later, when the sick were well and the wounded healed, he would ask the Great Father to permit their return to Wyoming Powder River country that had been their home.

Little Wolf, the practical realist, regretted Dull Knife's decision. "My brother, you can go into the agency if you wish; but I intend to work my way up to the Powder River country. I think it will be better for us all if the people are not divided."

But Dull Knife shook his head, and the matter was settled.

After the split-up, Little Wolf and his band kept on moving until they were deep into the desolate Sand Hills. Far back in that remote area, the winter was a happy time for the people of Little Wolf. No soldiers came hunting them, and game was plentiful. Meat simmered in the cooking pots every day and the women sang and laughed in the warm tepees. The children grew sleek and strong again, and their mothers made fine new garments for them from the skins of the many deer and antelope the hunters brought into camp.

It was a good time indeed; yet Little Wolf sat much alone, smoking his pipe and staring gloomily into his lodge-fire. The chief remembered something that his people, in their new-found happiness, had forgotten: the grim fact that with spring and melting snows would come the soldiers as before, hunting them down as wolves hunt the deer. Little Wolf was somberly aware that this good winter of ample food and warmth and much happiness could be but a bright interlude in the dark fate of the Cheyennes unless he alone could find a way to avert the catastrophe.

By the time March's warming sun had begun to melt the safeguarding snows, Little Wolf had made his difficult decision. He would lead his band far to the north across the invisible line in the earth that marked off the country of the Red Coats and the wise Grandmother beyond the seas who did not harry and destroy her red children. There, in the justly ruled land where Sitting Bull and his hunted Sioux had found sanctuary, he would seek a similar haven for the Cheyennes.

Quickly, then, the buffalo-skin lodges came down, the ponies were packed with lodge-poles, kettles, robes, and blankets; and the Indians again were on the move. The flankers and the warriors guarding the rear of the diminished village rode to their appointed positions; Little Wolf took the lead.

Northwest to the Powder River country the Cheyennes traveled, and it was here, in their home territory, that something occurred that drastically changed the chief's plans. Lieutenant W. P. Clark, chief of scouts at Fort Keogh on the Yellowstone River, came to the Indians' camp at sunset one evening bearing the heartening message that Bear Coat (General Nelson A. Miles) himself wished to talk peace with Little Wolf at

141

the fort. Clark was known to Little Wolf, and the chief listened carefully to his words. The lieutenant—also known as White Hat to the Cheyennes—talked earnestly and well: "I have prayed to the Great Spirit that I might find my friend Little Wolf, and now I have done so. I have come to you as a friend; I want you people to turn over your arms and go with me to Fort Keogh."

Many pipes were smoked before Little Wolf decided to forsake his plan of fleeing to Canada and accept General Miles's invitation to come to the fort for a parley. Once the chief's mind was made up the Cheyennes journeyed straight to Fort Keogh, where Miles greeted them warmly.

The bluff general, who was known and respected by all the Plains tribes as one soldier-chief who spoke with a straight tongue, shook hands heartily with Little Wolf. "You and I have been fighting each other a long time," said Miles. "Now, today, we meet and shake hands and will always be friends. I want you to give me all your horses. Then we will eat and sleep and talk again tomorrow." The chief agreed to this and told his people to turn over all their horses to General Miles. They obeyed, giving him every horse they had.

Next day, the general and Little Wolf met again, and Miles suggested that the chief and his warriors enlist with the army as scouts to help the soldiers round up the remnants of the defeated Sioux nation yet on American soil. But Little Wolf was not to be rushed into making a hasty decision. "My friend," he answered, "I have been traveling and fighting for a long time now, and I am tired. I do not like this at present."

General Miles, a shrewd judge of Indian character, did not press the weary war chief. "Very well," he replied, "think the matter over and see how you feel about it."

Little Wolf rested for three days, talking the matter over with his warriors. He didn't think much of Miles's offer himself, but his young men eagerly welcomed a chance to get even with the Sioux for failing to support them in a campaign of vengeance upon the soldiers after their bitter defeat by General Mackenzie and Major North. The chief yielded to the majority, and enlisted with Miles. Bear Coat's diplomacy and knowledge of Indian psychology had won out.

Tragically different was the fate of Dull Knife and his band. At White Clay Creek the chief had turned westward in the direction of Red Cloud Agency and Fort Robinson. Unfortunately, the agency had been abandoned while the Cheyennes had been exiled in the south. Confused by this unexpected development, Dull Knife moved on to Fort Robinson and surrendered to the commander there, Captain Wessels.

For two months the Cheyennes lived uneasily at the fort while Captain Wessels awaited orders from Washington. The orders arrived finally in the form of a curt telegram from the Indian Bureau: "Send the Cheyennes back to Darlington."

The C.O. sent for Dull Knife at once and informed him of the government's decision. The chief indignantly refused to accept it. "We will not go back there to live. That is not a healthful country; if we should stay there, we would all die. We do not wish to go back there, and we will not go."

Through an interpreter, Wessels replied: "It is not for you to say what you will or will not do. I have my orders from the Great Father. Tell your people to get ready to move south at once."

Dull Knife did not falter. He answered steadily, "No, I am here on my own ground, and I will never go back. You may kill me here, but you cannot make me go back!"

For a week Captain Wessels hammered away at the chief, trying to make him change his mind. Always Dull Knife refused. Finally, Wessels lost patience with the "stubborn old fool" and ordered all the Indians into a freezing barracks, with neither food nor water. At the end of three days the captain invited the women and children to come out of the barracks, leaving their men behind until they "got some sense in their heads." The women ignored the C.O.'s offer.

Cheyenne-speaking interpreters induced Wild Hog, Crow, and Strong Left Hand to come out of the barracks by promising them food and good treatment. Once outside the door, they were seized and dragged to the guardhouse. Wild Hog drew his knife and tried to commit suicide. While the soldiers were struggling with him, Strong Left Hand escaped and dashed back to the barracks, yelling: "They have got Wild Hog; they are going to handcuff him!"

"Now," said Dull Knife to his warriors, "dress yourselves in your best clothes and sing your death-songs, for we must prepare to die!"

For three more days the Cheyennes remained in the barracks without heat, food, or water in below-zero weather. Some of the old men became delirious and babbled of ancient buffalo hunts and hoary battles against the Assiniboines and the Pawnees. The children grew so frantic for water they scraped away all the snow that had collected on the window ledges. Women kept up a continual low moaning, and sleep was impossible for anyone except the utterly exhausted.

On the third day, Captain Wessels—speaking through his interpreter—gave the Cheyennes their "last chance" to give up and go south. Dull Knife replied, weakly but firmly: "We will not go. The only way to get us there is to come in with clubs and knock us on the head and drag us out and take us down there dead. We have nothing to defend ourselves with, and if you want to you can come in here with clubs and kill us all like dogs."

At sunset of January 9, 1879, Little Shield, the Dog

Soldier chief of the band, said to the others: "Now the time has come for us to die like Cheyennes and not like foxes in a trap. Make yourselves ready, for tonight we will break out of here and run for the hills!"

Near dusk the break was made. Little Shield led the way, having first assembled the few guns and revolvers the Dog Soldiers had managed to hide piecemeal in the clothing of the women and children. Little Shield's first shot killed a guard patrolling near the barracks, and at the signal, warriors smashed the window sashes and leaped out shooting. The others followed; all ran for the hills with the soldiers chasing them.

The old men and women and the children were the first to be killed, since they could not run as fast as the others. Some of the Indians stopped to drink at a half-frozen stream. Many were killed there. The water turned bloody.

Fifty Cheyennes died in the crimsoned snow on that moonlit bitter-cold night of January 9, 1879, before the kill-crazed troopers stopped shooting. Twenty more died of wounds and exposure before the dazed survivors were rounded up and thrown back into the barracks.

Among the few to escape were Dull Knife and his wife and son, who hid in a great hole in the rocks until the soldiers gave up hunting them. Later, under cover of darkness, the chief and his family got away to the Pine Ridge Sioux Agency by traveling at night for eighteen nights. They ate bark and roots and finally their own moccasins before reaching Pine Ridge. More dead than alive, they crept up to Bill Rowland's cabin and knocked feebly on the interpreter's door. Rowland took them in, fed them, treated their frost-bitten hands and feet, and later arranged for their permanent residence at the agency.

Thirty-one warriors fled into the broken hills beyond Fort Robinson and fought a hopeless running engagement with Wessels' troopers for six days before being wiped out. They made their last stand in a washout among the Hat Creek Bluffs, many of them wounded, most of them half-frozen, and all exhausted and starving.

Wessels ringed the gully with three hundred troopers and called upon the Cheyennes to surrender. Three shots were his answer—the last three cartridges left in the Cheyenne rifles. The troops advanced, firing. Three Dog Soldiers rose out of the gully to meet them: all that were left alive of the thirty-one. They had no more ammunition, so they clubbed their empty guns and charged: three against three hundred. The soldiers shot them to pieces.

So it ended, in a bloody gully in the Hat Creek Bluffs, the epic fight for freedom of the Cheyennes.

The Peace Messiah. *Montage by John Kress*

THE PEACE
MESSIAH

by Sharon S. and Thomas W. McKern

*B*y 1888, the buffalo were
gone from the American plains. The ugly specter of
starvation, once an apparition deftly banished, loomed
now a harsh reality kept at bay only be meager *wasi-
chu* rations of rancid bacon and weevily flour. Even
these decreased with every census; as the relentless
epidemics swept the plains, decimating tribal numbers,
the Indians began to falsify their head-counts in a desperate attempt to stave off further ration cuts.

After a decade of reservation life, there remained
among them no children who remembered the sight of
great grazing herds or the smell of juicy ribs, split and
cracking over open fires. The days of spontaneous,
high-spirited games and careless gossip were ended.
The women fell silent, grieving after infants fast lost to
rampant onslaughts of disease and infection. The men,

bereft of the pride and purpose that came with hunting, sat dazed and listless before the dark log cabins. Like their women they waited, helpless witnesses to the slow grinding-down of Indian resistance.

For a people overwhelmed by powerful alien forces, there exist but two alternatives: resist, or surrender. Seldom does there remain strength of leadership equal to the former course—yet seldom can the latter be borne. And so very often there occurs instead a vast revival of ancient faith and an anguished outcry for one in whom that faith might be vested: a great, benevolent, omnipotent messiah who will pluck up and cast out the seeds of creeping destruction and restore a happier world.

Inevitably, a redeemer—self-appointed—appears. And he is welcomed, for few people caught in the throes of cultural crisis can resist the soothing words of a messiah pledged to deliver religious relief to defeat's throbbing agonies. It is a phenomenon common in history.

For the Indians of the American West, the messiah would come in the guise of Wovoka, a Paiute medicine man bred to the working of the occult. Acting upon instructions revealed to him in a fever-induced trance, Wovoka brought to the dying nations of nineteenth-century America a long-awaited prophecy of redemption. Promising a regenerated earth and an end to white domination, Wovoka advocated a revolutionary new code of Indian conduct firmly based upon the principles of peace and forebearance, and forbidding violence in any form. His teaching, strongly reminiscent of the Christian influence to which he was exposed as a young man and enhanced by a few minor miracles well within the range of his talents as an able shaman, bound together the seldom-united tribes of the West and delivered to them one last great hope for survival.

That this hope would prove ultimately futile diminishes not at all the eminence of this single self-appoint-

*Wovoka, the Paiute "Peace Messiah" (right) at the
height of his influence*

ed redeemer who, ambitious for himself and for his people, achieved an almost mystic revival of Indian faith. Through his prophecies the essential elements of Christianity and paganism were joined to culminate in the establishment, across the land, of nativistic cults, centering about the *wana ghi wa chipi*—the ghost dance. Ironically, it would be the dance, that hypnotic manifestation of Wovoka's incessant demand for non-violence, that would lead to the bloodiest of massacres at Wounded Knee and evoke the final death spasms of the once-mighty Sioux nation. Wovoka was uniquely qualified to assume the role of messiah. Born about 1856, he was the son of Tavibo, a Paiute mystic so revered for his prophecies that his fame vaulted tribal boundaries. From his earliest years, Wovoka accompanied his father as Tavibo plied a magician's trade: divining, healing, providing for his people a living link between the natural and supernatural.

Such a spiritual go-between is mandatory among such people as the Paiute. The primitive world is a dangerous one, richly peopled with spirits both good and evil. There worship is never confined to a sabbath; religion permeates all facets of daily life. In a world riotous with non-human voices (and where every human action bears a spiritual consequence) it could not be otherwise.

The Indian lives in intimate relationship with his dead ancestors and with his surroundings; not only ghosts but also animals, trees, rocks, streams, even the planets, are soul-filled. Each maintains a constant and alert interest in the affairs of man and expects to play an active role in the course of human events. Every spirit must be dealt with, its wishes interpreted, its occasional ire appeased. For within the primitive mind lurks the unassailable certainty that each illness has its spiritual origin, each disaster its spiritual key.

Only in magic can a cause for each be divined, and

only through magic can a cure be effected. Magic, witchcraft, divination, prophecy, curing—these are the tasks that fall to the shaman. Matters too critical for the ordinary layman, these must be entrusted to a specialist. For the Paiute, such tasks came to Tavibo, the designated tribal middleman whose job it was to link the living with the non-living and with the dead—and so ensure Paiute survival.

Tavibo, master of the occult, tended for many years the spiritual affairs of his tribe. Recognizing in his son the gift of vision, Tavibo planned that Wovoka would fall heir to his position as tribal visionary. The young Paiute served a lengthy apprenticeship, mastering first the small tricks, the ventriloquism and sleight of hand that, like the ever-present hide medicine bundle, distinguish a skillful shaman. Later came intensive instruction in the complexities of spirit language, in the exercise of magic in healing, and in the intricacies of prophecy, that mysterious art by which spirit-given visions are interpreted by certain gifted men for the benefit and protection of their people.

Tavibo was a patient teacher bent on passing to his son a prestigious position of tribal leadership; Wovoka was a receptive pupil, possessed of a clear and certain calling. His was a heritage rich in the ancient rites that manifest a faith to which he was from birth deeply committed.

Wovoka would encounter the trappings of other faiths, and each would lend subtle direction to the course of his destiny. With the death of Tavibo, Wovoka—not yet a man—was taken in by David Wilson, a white rancher, and his wife. From the Wilsons, Wovoka accepted, perhaps indifferently, his white name, Jack Wilson.

From them, too, he learned of the white god, awesome source of alien power. Each evening after supper, the Wilsons read aloud from their single Bible; like an ambassador learning the customs of a land in which he must temporarily be housed, Wovoka listened intently, asking at the reading's end quiet, perceptive questions.

The Paiute puzzled over the curious fact that the whites, rich in so many other ways, possessed but one god, ignoring the numerous other powers of good and evil that so dominate the Indian universe. He admired the perplexing Jesus, a medicine man so powerful that he could effect miraculous cures without the aid of animal helpers and create food where there was none before—and yet choose to offer no resistance when, betrayed, he was led to his death on a cross. Stoicism was a quality the Paiute could admire.

Certain other elements of Christianity stirred Wovoka's imagination. The biblical account of Jesus' resurrection, the prophecies of a second coming and the hope these generated, the stories of good rewarded, these seemed to him compelling tales worthy of his attention. He would never forget them; they would emerge from his memory later in a form uniquely pagan.

Wovoka's close association with the Wilsons persisted for almost two decades. His relationship with the Wilson children ripened into friendship, and he extended them a cautious affection. On one occasion—when Wovoka had promised to demonstrate his magic by making ice appear in the river on a summer afternoon —the Wilson boys turned prophecy to fact by racing upstream to dump ice blocks in the water.

But Wovoka never adopted the white world. He chose to visit there only in balancing his ledger, for he was meticulous in earning his keep by tending the white man's chores. Short and rotund, oddly handsome, Wovoka dispatched these with quiet dignity; his back was willing, his hands agile, but his heart and mind were reserved for the Paiute of Mason Valley. His true work lay in magic and prophecy.

Wovoka with T. J. (Tim?) McCoy in 1926.
Wovoka was seventy years of age and all but forgotten.

The death of old Tavibo had left no void in the lives of the Paiute; even in mourning Wovoka accepted the responsibility for curing the illnesses of his people and for guiding their relationships with the supernatural. These were perilous times. The Paiute had never known true abundance; a marginal people, they failed even in the past to share with stronger tribes the wealth of the plains.

Now, pushed by white settlement into the most barren of Nevada wastelands, they scarcely managed to sustain life. For much of the year, they subsisted on roots and berries, taking an occasional windfall of protein from snares hidden in the desert—snakes, lizards, desert mice. The killing of a rabbit or deer was an event to provoke the most frenzied excitement. For the Paiute, life's mainstay was not food but spiritual promise; and this, in the face of abysmal and relentless poverty, was wearing thin. They looked to Wovoka to find a way of staying the tide of white infiltration and secure for them more favorable lands.

But Wovoka had no magic that would restore a vanished world. Sharing with his people a crippling sense of loss and despair, Wovoka feared in the wake of invading whites and in the meanness of the innumerable petty restrictions imposed by blue-coated authorities a total collapse of the ancient framework of beliefs that in the past sustained the Paiute. Too realistic to imagine possible a return to the old ways, Wovoka, nevertheless, saw no profit for his people in adopting the ways of the alien newcomers; Christianity offered no respite to the crumbling of long-held tribal values, no reprieve from the apathy and confusion that now enveloped not only the Paiute but also the neighboring Shoshoni and Bannock.

Too long an Indian to relinquish his faith in the supernatural, Wovoka knew that the answer must come from the spirits and he prayed for a vision that would reveal to him the course he must pursue to lead his people from despair to triumph. Although the spirits continued to aid him in his practice of magic and medicine, this single answer was withheld: the spirits sent no illuminating vision.

In the meantime, life must be sustained. Wovoka seldom wandered far from the place of his birth, and even at the peak of his power, as acknowledged spiritual leader for all the Indians of the West, he would remain with his people. During this time of agonizing need, however, he would leave the tribe, reluctantly hiring himself out to whites who would pay in dollars and gold, paltry sums, but sufficient for the purchase of supplies that would supplement the meager Paiute diet. It was a rare journey to the West Coast that provided Wovoka the answer he sought. Working temporarily in the hop fields near Puget Sound, the young Paiute encountered again and again newly formed Shaker cults founded by the Squaxon Indian, John Slocum.

Slocum's followers practiced a crude but enthusiastic mixture of Christianity and witchcraft dominated in ceremony by trance ritual. These were religious elements intimately known to Wovoka, but combined here in persuasive new form. He took the trouble to learn the essentials of Shaker doctrine, participating in more than a few of the frenzied trance ceremonies.

In the end, Wovoka would reject the Shaker faith, finding in it no solution to the problem of disease and hunger that plagued the Nevada Paiute. But he had noted the remarkable regenerating effect the practice of this strange religion had upon its followers, particularly among the newest converts. At a time when Indian spirits across the continent sagged in blackest gloom, the Shakers led a life both joyous and exuberant. Wovoka had learned, perhaps unconsciously, how effectively the components of diverse faiths can be combined to evoke a powerful new religion in which

155

The Ghost Dance of the Aprapaho. The Arapahoes were ardent supporters of Wovoka.

devastated people can rediscover strength and spiritual direction. Nor did it escape his notice that the cult's founder enjoyed status and prestige far exceeding that usual for the most gifted of medicine men.

Wovoka left the lushness of Puget Sound, returning to the barren lands of his people only to find that conditions, never good, were now disastrous. Hunger, humiliation, and disease had taken an ugly toll; for the dazed survivors there was no resiliency left in mind or in body. The old life lay vulnerable to slow but certain disintegration.

In December, Wovoka himself fell victim to a severe infection, one of the score that stalked the camp. Confined to a pallet in his wickiup, he lay for weeks in a feverish coma, weak, disoriented, often delirious. His fever raged unabated until January 1, 1889. It was on this day that Wovoka experienced the vision for which he had prayed: the vision that would alter the course of Plains history. Prophetically, it was on this day too that the Indians of Mason Valley witnessed a miracle unparalleled in Paiute legend: a total eclipse of the sun.

Nothing in their experience prepared Wovoka's people for the phenomenon of solar eclipse. For them, laid vulnerable by the prolonged illness of their sole spiritual advisor, this was a day of incredible horror. At one moment, the sun shone clear and bright. In the next a great shadow threatened its face. The Paiute recoiled in terror, certain that before their eyes the sun, most revered of all Indian dieties, would be devoured by a fierce and malevolent spirit. The ensuing gloom, inexplicable in the middle of day, plunged them into unprecedented panic.

As if with a single thought, they acted in the only course available to them: they shouted, clanged together their dried gourds, fired their few guns into the air —anything to create a din sufficiently fearsome to drive away the beast that sought to consume their sun. When seemingly they succeeded, for the sun emerged whole and triumphant, their joy was unbounded. They were not, after all, doomed to lose what little was left of their world to a frightening and eternal darkness.

Soon Wovoka, his fever miraculously broken, walked among his people, and told of a great vision. When the sun died, he said, Wovoka had died too, and journeyed to the heavens where he talked with God. Now like the sun he lived again, an emissary chosen by God to return to earth the bearer of glad tidings. The heavens, Wovoka said, were peopled not with white men, but with the souls of Indian tribesmen. And what a heaven it was: there was permitted there no hunger or disease, no agony of aged bones grown weak, no memory of defeat or domination. The Paiute spirits lived in peace and harmony with those of other tribes—the Sioux, Shoshoni, Bannock, Arapaho, even the mortally fierce Apache. All were free of pain, eternally free from need.

Wovoka described heaven's ruler in striking resemblance to the god of David Wilson's Bible. But Wovoka's god had been betrayed by the white man. He belonged now to the Paiute. This god promised a new millennium: the white man's god would reappear on earth but this time in Indian garb, to bring salvation to the Paiute and to their brothers across the land. He would end white domination, rolling the invaders like a giant wave back across the ocean to the distant lands from which they came. The streams would flow clear and cool. The buffalo would return; the lands would come alive with game. The revived souls of dead tribesmen would walk the earth in happy reunion with their mortal brothers. Sickness and hunger would recede into memory. All this Wovoka had seen in his vision. All this would come to pass, a gift from a messiah who would come soon from the west in the flesh of an Indian.

Mary I. Wright's version of the Arapaho Ghost Dance

In the meantime, the Indians must honor a Christian god's laws. They must lead lives of virtue, honesty, industry and peace. There would be no more lying, no theft. Above all else, there must be no fighting. Violence of any kind was forbidden; no harm must be done to any person, white or red. And the Indians must dance the *dance-in-a-circle*, brought by Wovoka from heaven.

Wovoka was hardly the first in history to promise, through prophecy, a regenerated world. More than a century before, the Ottawa chief Pontiac, guided by the visions of an Indian mystic whose name is lost to us, almost succeeded in driving the British from Ohio and reclaiming tribal lands. Tecumseh, directed by the prophecies of his shaman brother Laulewasika, waged a mighty campaign for a return to the old ways and an end to white settlement. Later, Handsome Lake, an Iroquois medicine man, deftly combined the elements of Christianity and paganism to form the basis of a new faith, a religion that united his people and gave them the will to survive in the face of ceaseless white domination.

Nor is the messianic phenomenon confined to North America. James Mooney, the only trained anthropologist to witness at first hand the spread of ghost dance cults, argued that the establishment of such nativistic sects was inevitable among oppressed people. He compared the doctrine of Wovoka with those of the Hindu avatar, with the Hebrew messiah, and with the white Christ, writing that they "are essentially the same, and have their origin in a hope and longing common to all humanity." All groups struggle against fearsome odds to preserve their cultural and spiritual heritage. When there remains no strength for force, it is to worship that they turn, led by those who claim an intimacy with the gods. Inevitably, it is here that they find the will to endure.

For the Paiute, devoid of hope for more than a generation, Wovoka's message was a joyous one. The new commandments were strange, the injunction against fighting unprecedented in Paiute lore. But there would be no doubting the truth of Wovoka's message: he was the son of Tavibo and at the moment of his vision, there had occurred an awesome omen, the sky-battle between the powers of light and darkness. The triumph of the solar deity clearly presaged better times in store for the faithful Paiute; Wovoka's message merely confirmed what could not be false.

Hope rekindled, the Paiute of Mason Valley set about at once to learn the ritualized *dance-in-a-circle* prescribed by Wovoka. Many of those who danced were transported in religious ecstasy to the world of the supernatural, where they mingled with the ghosts of lost tribesmen and walked among the vanished game.

The message was too joyous to be contained; Indians who had learned to write acted now as scribes for those less acculturated. Paiutes riding the rails to visit relatives in distant reservations carried the word. Soon tales of Wovoka's prophecy swept the West like a firestorm, together with the testimony of those who had danced and talked with long-dead tribesmen. Word of Wovoka's teaching penetrated the boundaries of almost every reservation west of the Mississippi.

Indian delegations began to trickle into Mason Valley as if toward Mecca as far-flung tribes sent emissaries to investigate rumors of a Paiute able to resurrect the dead. Here they learned the rituals requisite to the performance of the sacred dance, but only after hearing Wovoka's repeated admonitions against violence: "Do not fight. Deliver no violence against anyone. Do good always."

The Shoshoni and Bannock were present at the first Paiute dance, adopting it immediately. The Mohave and Walapai took the dance too, directly from the

The Ghost Dance of the Ogallala Sioux as drawn by Frederic Remington

Paiute, duplicating the ritual even to the Paiute song-language with which they were familiar. The Caddo, Wichita, and Delaware, confined to the poorest lands of Oklahoma, learned the dance from the Arapaho, among the first of the Plains tribes to embrace the new doctrine. As its most ardent supporters, the Arapaho would carry the dance east. The Shoshoni at Fort Hall Reservation in Idaho, almost straddling the Great Divide, would spread the word both east and west.

Delegates who visited Wovoka at Mason Valley returned home to report great amazing miracles. Many witnessed the return of the lost buffalo. Others had talked with the spirits. For those who doubted, Wovoka demonstrated his powers, producing rainfall in the midst of drought. Reports began to circulate that Wovoka controlled the elements, ordering rain or snow and delivering it on demand. From obscurity, Wovoka rose to prominence, his name a whispered chant of renewed hope.

A few tribes located near the center of the new religious activity never adopted the dance. Peoples of the Great Columbia Basin, strongly influenced by both Catholic and Protestant missionaries, rejected Wovoka's teaching. The Comanches, inherently distrustful, refused to acknowledge any gods not their own. The Navaho, still possessed of healthy herds and a certain wealth in silver, initially resisted the peace movement. But later, rumors of resurrected dead piqued their interest and, in the latter part of 1890 when Mexicans and Americans began to encroach upon tribal lands, some Navahos hastened to learn the dance and join in the waiting for the new millennium.

The dance and the doctrine spread wherever the old life was threatened. Recalling a free-ranging life of hunting from Mexico to the Dakotas, tribes now confined to reservations chafed under white restrictions; they found direction in the teachings of Wovoka and eagerly adopted the dance he prescribed. Incidents of Indian harrassment of white settlers dwindled; Wovoka demanded peace. Embracing for the first time a Christian ethic, the Indians exhibited a most unchristian tolerance for those who ridiculed their new religious efforts. Those who performed the *dance-in-a-circle* raised no hand in anger or violence.

Each tribe incorporated into the dance elements of its unique sacred lore. For the Paiute, the *dance-in-a-circle* was performed around a central pile of blazing logs. Among the Shoshoni, the *dance-of-everybody-dragging* encircled a small cedar tree. For the Sioux, the ritual was *wana ghi wa chipi,* the *ghost dance*.

As the dance spread, it evolved into divergent forms. Some groups would omit the "giving of the feather," that preparatory step which concedes to the leader the right to direct the dance. Others would substitute an eagle's feather for that of the crow, sacred to the Paiute dance. Some tribes added at the dance's end the debilitating sweat bath; others would prolong the preliminary fasting, increasing the chances of trance induction. In each tribe, the body paint of the participants would vary even among individuals as each would carry into the dance symbols sacred to him. Most common were elaborate designs in red, yellow, green and blue—of solar discs, crescents, stars, crosses, and crows.

What was common to all forms of the dance was the exhausting duration of the performance itself, lasting as long as four days and four nights, and the psychological responses it elicited. The participant, weakened by fasting and fatigue, and hypnotized by the monotonous beat-and-chant of the rite, eventually succumbs to the power of religious fervor. His excitement builds to fever pitch, his eyes glaze; spurred on by the sight of bodies dropping around him, he dances until such agitation can no longer be tolerated. And then he falls to

*The Arapaho ghost shirt. The Sioux felt that such
shirts would protect them from the bullets of the whites*

the ground, limbs rigid, lapsing into the trance so ardently sought. He may lay unconscious, untouched, for many hours before awakening to tell of his trance-vision. It is through the trance the Indian validates his religious experience. What comes in a vision is not to be doubted.

The vision, filtered through the precepts of ancient tribal lore, emerges to reflect not only a vindication of Wovoka's prophecy but also a new and tribally unique interpretation of the peace thinking. Just as the teachings of Christ provided the basis for the founding of numerous divergent beliefs, so did the words of the Paiute Wovoka lend themselves to scores of related doctrines. Delegates dispatched to Nevada returned to their people to describe Wovoka in terms of their own experiences; each tribe pursued the new millennium upon its own terms.

It was in this way that Wovoka, the peace messiah, was transformed into a messenger of death.

Most of the tribal misinterpretations of Wovoka's doctrine involved imaginative elaborations on the theme of a messiah coming. The Shoshoni of Wyoming predicted a deep sleep, during which a cataclysm would transform the earth and after which the Indians could live peaceably with the whites. The Cheyenne preferred to believe that a repopulated Indian world would be raised up by the sacred crow, leaving the white men below, isolated but unharmed. It was the Cheyenne who first contended that it was Wovoka himself who came as a messiah; as the son of God, they claimed Wovoka displayed upon his body the marks of an ancient crucifixion. The latter rumor spread, becoming an integral part of the ghost dance legend. But it is believed that Wovoka never represented himself as the son of God.

Nevertheless, numerous Indian tribes and many whites believed Wovoka to represent Christ in his second coming. This belief was strengthened by the prophecy of the Mormon founder Joseph Smith, Jr., who in 1843 had predicted that a messiah would come to earth in the year 1890. For the Mormons living then in the region, the American Indians represented the descendants of the lost tribes of Israel, the true *Lamanites* who wandered into the western hemisphere before the time of Christ. It seemed logical to them that the promised son of God would appear in Indian guise.

Even as the other tribes elaborated upon Wovoka's prophecy, the Sioux devised their own interpretations, including a small distinction that would transform Wovoka's doctrine of non-violence into a prophecy of blood and vengeance. While the other tribes, according to Wovoka's teaching, awaited a messiah who would bring salvation to the Indian, the Sioux awaited a redeemer who would bring revenge against the white man.

Seven Sioux delegates visited Mason Valley early in 1890; several of them participating in the dance, and experienced visions in which they talked with long-dead relatives. They received the same careful teaching from Wovoka given to the other delegates—a never-changing admonition against violence—but when the delegates returned to the Sioux, they carried a message of revenge.

Wovoka was the true son of God, they said, proven so by the scars he bore upon his limbs; he was sent by God to punish the whites not only for killing Jesus but also for their sins against the Indians. By the spring of 1894, Wovoka would carry God's wrath across the plains, ridding the earth of the hated whites. Vengeance would come to the Sioux. They need only wait, performing in the meantime the sacred dance. Soon there would be peace and plenty.

The distortion would prove a fatal one, but hardly a surprising one. For the Sioux were restless and fearful;

171

even closer to the brink of destruction than their neighboring tribes, they had been driven to barren lands rejected or unclaimed by white settlers. Forbidden to hunt, they turned to agriculture. The summer of 1890 brought with the most severe drought in American history. No rain fell; hot prairie winds and blistering sun beat down their poor crops. Weakened by disease and hunger, the Sioux were dependent upon government rations.

The census, always a humiliating experience, proved now a fearful one, as rations were cut again and again on the basis of high mortality rates. Behind the Sioux lay a decade of broken promises and unsettled boundary disputes; ahead stretched a vision of slow, agonizing years of despair, unless a messiah rose up to strike down their enemies and restore the vanished game. They began, in earnestness born of desperation, to perform the ghost dance.

Another Sioux innovation was added at this time. Certain that white aggression would erupt against them before the arrival of the promised messiah, they turned to native medicine for immunity from harm. The device—preventive medicine—was the *ghost shirt*, perhaps inspired by the Mormon endowment robe.

Patterned after a shirt seen in a vision, the garment was heavily adorned with painted symbols, sewn with sinew and decoratively fringed. The designs were inscribed with sacred red paint; the feathers were crow and eagle, both sacred to the dance. The shirts were said to be impenetrable by the white man's bullets. They were worn not only by the warriors, but by tribal women and children also, persuasive evidence that the Sioux intended not to make war (for in that case they would have chosen war paint) but to seek protection against white aggression and betrayal.

The Sioux were impatient, even with such immunity from harm. In October of 1890, Short Bull, the most fervent of ghost dance advocates, advanced the date of deliverance, predicting that the new messiah would come within a month. They instigated no violence, but they talked of swift revenge. Rumors spread of an imminent Indian uprising.

The agents of Sioux reservations—Standing Rock and Pine Ridge in particular—were unnerved by the constant dancing and ritual, and advised the War Department to give credence to rumors of uprising. In November, more than three thousand government field troops arrived in the Dakotas. Scores of Sioux warriors panicked, fleeing into the badlands with their women and children. Isolated incidents of hostility began to threaten the uneasy peace.

The great chief Sitting Bull, urged toward action by progressive hostiles, chose instead a stoic attitude of watchful waiting. He had no faith in the ghost dance doctrine. He was too long a Sioux to accept the garbled precepts of Christianity on which the cult was based. Unsuccessful in his attempts to lapse into a trance and so visit with his beloved dead daughter, and admonished not to dance by government agents, he played a passive role in the cult, refusing to participate but refusing also to force his people to forfeit the means by which they hoped to bring salvation.

The extraordinary military scrutiny under which the Sioux lived that autumn began to gnaw at the confidence of other, more progressive leaders. Nerves made tense by ten years of inadequate rations and the recent crop failure drew taut and raw; only a spark was needed to turn deep resentment into flaming protest. Had Congress seen fit at this time to restore previous ration cuts, the dance cult may have run its harmless course. But Congress was occupied with weightier matters. The Sioux were left to the mercy of local agents and ill-informed troop commanders.

Receiving now a flood of communications reporting

Sioux restlessness, the Commissioner of Indian Affairs pressed for further information. Complaints were filed against the more progressive Sioux leaders. Ironically, the white agents focused their attention upon Sitting Bull, the acknowledged leader of the extensive Sioux nation. In December, orders were transmitted to arrest Sitting Bull.

Nemerous police officers resigned, flatly rejecting any duty that involved the arrest of so revered a chief. Police from surrounding reservations were dispatched instead, entering Sitting Bull's cabin on the Standing Rock reservation under the protection of heavy armament. The old chief dressed quietly, submitting peaceably to arrest.

But an excited, nervous throng had gathered before Sitting Bull's cabin. There are several versions of what happened next. A shot was fired and in the melee that followed Sitting Bull was killed by Bullhead and Red Tomahawk, both Indian police. When the shooting was over eight Indians and six Indian police lay dead in front of Sitting Bull's cabin.

The ghost shirts held no magic two weeks later at Wounded Knee when nearly two hundred of Big Foot's band of Sioux men, women and children were slain on December 29, 1890. It was here, at Wounded Knee, that the final hope of the Sioux was ended, and with it the faith of surrounding tribes in the coming of a new millennium.

The dancing continued in a few isolated outposts, but most tribes, fearful under increased military scrutiny, desisted. Many blamed the Sioux for crushing, through reckless talk of revenge, the last hope of Indian America. When the messiah failed to appear in 1891, doubt solidified into rejection of the peace doctrine. The endless trek to Mason Valley was stilled. Wovoka, saddened by the fate of the Sioux and by the failure of the messiah to appear on schedule, meditated, waiting for a new vision that would illuminate his "misinterpretation" of his visit to heaven in 1889. When he died in obscurity in 1932, only the Paiute surrounded him.

The dancing continues today among a handful of tribes, evidence that deliverance has yet to come, either through the acts of their gods or the efforts of their conquerors—and mute testimony to the need, still critical, for a devastated people to find their place in an uncertain future.

Sitting Bull

A mask of the False Face Society

HUMOR
OF THE
AMERICAN
INDIAN

by Robert Easton

*A*ll Indians are stoic, stolid and devoid of humor." This is firmly believed by that great mass of white people who have never known any Indians. This misconception is even shared by some Indian "experts," including: Michigan matrons who have actually purchased authentic Indian artifacts from authentic Indians during five minute railroad stops in Nothern New Mexico; men of the cloth dedicated to replacing such grossly materialistic heathen notions as the "Great Spirit" with such spiritually exalted concepts as "hellfire and brimstone," and minor government bureaucrats sent to reason with recalcitrant redskins and rationalize repeated violations of treaty rights granted by earlier Great White Fathers during foolish fits of philanthropy.

Despite what most white people think, American Indians enjoy a rich legacy of laughter. The marked disparity between common belief and the facts was explained as early as 1882 by Col. Richard Irving Dodge in his *Our Wild Indians—Thirty-three Years' Personal Experience Among the Red Men of the Great West.* Col. Dodge's analysis of the Indian: "In the presence of strangers he is reserved and silent . . . The general impression seems to be that the Indian, wrapped in his blanket and impenetrable mystery, and with a face of gloom, stalks through life unmindful of pleasure or pain. Nothing can be farther from the truth. The dignity, the reserve, the silence, are put on just as a New York swell puts on his swallow-tailed coat and white choker for a dinner party, because it is his custom. In his own camp, away from strangers, the Indian is a noisy, jolly, rollicking, mischief-loving braggadocio, brimful of practical jokes and rough fun of any kind making the welkin ring with his laughter."

If Col. Dodge's explanation seems too 19th century for your tastes, here's a late-model 20th century analysis from *Pattern in Cultural Anthropology* by Melville Jacobs: "Americans are . . . so fearful and serious that it seems as if they have perpetuated an almost classic projection in their grim-faced great-grandparents' stereotype of an invariably dour Plains Indian. Ethnographers have learned, the time consuming way, that Plains and almost all other American Indians were as prone as any peoples to quip and giggle except in the presence of those whom they distrusted and disliked."

Even the most trusted and sympathetic of ethnographers ran into difficulties when they tried to tackle Indian humor. As William J. Wallace pointed out in his article "The Role of Humor in the Hupa Indian Tribe" (Journal of American Folk-Lore, Vol. 66, No. 260), "It is exceedingly hard for a fieldworker to become sufficiently acquainted with the people he is studying to comprehend the nature of this faculty because its understanding presupposes a feeling for the finest shades of meaning in tribal culture, language, and psychology. This is rarely, if ever, acquired by an outsider."

Many of the mirth-making items detailed in the two best surveys in the field—Wallace's article on Hupa humor, and W. W. Hill's monograph "Navaho Humor" —would not necessarily provoke belly-laughs in pale-face circles. But Indian humor is not designed to amuse the white man. You have to understand tribal tabus and etiquette before you can laugh at the rascal or boor who violates them. Hill himself confesses: "The author has many times during the course of his field-work been the cause of a witticism because of some unconscious transgression of Navaho social form or action." Hill then goes on to detail how frequently the Navaho are amused by whites, giving such examples as: "Should a man assume the position of a woman with his legs under him or a woman sit cross-legged, the normal position of a Navaho man, humorous remarks are bound to follow."

As startling as it may seem to the white man, he has no monopoly on such ethnocentric notions as "The way *we* do it is normal; the way *they* do it is funny." Wallace comments on the Hupa in this regard: "The Whilkut and Chilula . . . were favorite targets. The Hupa thought them a somewhat backward and queer lot and told many illustrative stories. Their . . . dialect was a constant source of merriment . . . 'Everyone thought they acted strange and spoke funny.' "

Hill describes such traditional Navaho comic insults as calling one another Utes or Paiutes. He also tells us the proverbial Navaho comment for a social faux pas such as inadvertent "flatulation in mixed company" is "only the Pueblos do that."

In fact, each tribe savors its own rich store of comic-lore about the eccentricities of neighbouring tribes; but the culture collision with white society is the hot house in which Indian wit really bursts into full bloom.

In their *Homespun America* Brockway and Winer recount a famous example: "When gold was discovered in the Black Hills, then part of an Indian reservation, the government offered to lease the land from the Indians for a hundred years, paying only a nominal rental for mining privileges (the Indians were asking a purchase price of 60,000,000 dollars). The Sioux chief Spotted Tail, after a conference with the government agents, pointed to their mules: he didn't want to buy them, he said; only "borrow them—for a hundred years."

After being subjected to the repeated hardsell techniques of a proselytizing white preacher the Seneca chief Red Jacket pleasantly told him: "We are told that you have been preaching to the white people in this place . . . We will wait a little while, and see what effect your preaching has upon them. If we find it does them good, makes them honest and less disposed to cheat Indians, we will then consider again of what you have said."

Other "missionaries" wended their way westward telling Indians the good news that they were all wallowing in original sin. In his *American Folklore* Richard M. Dorson quotes the rebuff received by one of these worthies: "You come across the water to tell us you killed your god, and then you blame us for it." Dorson gives other examples of anti-clerical Indian wit, summarizing the process: "The comic Indian secures revenge on the white man who sneers at Indian myths as childish, by reducing the Christian myth to the same skeletal absurdity."

Dorson also recounts the classic tale of Hendrick, chief of the Mohawks and the British General, Sir William Johnson, but I prefer the variant oral version told me by Grey Otter (Skeeter Vaughan), the Cherokee tomahawk expert: One day the chief mentioned to the

British general, "You know last night I dreamed that I had a beautiful red coat like yours." One of the general's advisers whispered to him, "General, you better give him your coat. These Indians are very polite and they would never think of asking for anything; but it is their custom to say that they dreamed that they had it, and the the polite thing is for the other person to say 'I will make your dream come true' and give it to them." So the general gave the chief his beautiful red coat.

Some time later the general said to the chief, "You know last night I dreamed that you gave me all the land in this valley." The chief stared at him for a long moment and then said, "I will make your dream come true. The valley is yours."

Several months later the chief told the general, "You know that land I gave you? Last night I dreamed you gave it back."

The Sioux love to tell the story of the hatchet-faced white schoolmarm who demanded of her charges that they translate their Indian names into English for her roll call. Most of the names were innocuous enough until one little lad informed her his name was Johnny Shits-While-Running. She was about to punish him but the other Indian children assured her that really was the correct translation of his Sioux name. So she went to the chiefs and complained that she found the name Johnny Shits-While-Running offensive. She asked them to change Johnny's name and they agreed they would. In due course Johnny proudly told his teacher that his name had been officially changed so that it would no longer displease her. Inquiring what his new name was she was informed, "Johnny Does-Not-Shit-While-Running."

Babbitty bureaucrats and tourists who ask stupid questions are favorite targets of dead-pan redskin repartee. In *The Real Americans* A. Hyatt Verrill cites some droll examples:

" 'Is it true that you Indians eat dogs?' the tourist asked the young Pawnee. 'Yes, sir' replied the Indian, 'but good eatin' dogs is mighty scarce since the price of sausages has gone up.'

" 'Why don't you work?' demanded the white man. 'You can get a good job.' The Indian dozing in the sun glanced up. 'Why?' he muttered. 'So you can earn money,' replied the white man. 'If you save money and put it in the bank, by and by you will have enough so you won't have to work any more.' 'Huh,' replied the Indian, 'Me no work now.'

"Invited by a Dakota chief to stay overnight in his village, a white preacher anxiously asked whether his horse and saddle would be safe. 'Yes,' the chief reassured him, 'There isn't a white man within two days' ride of here.'

" 'What's your nationality?' the census-taker asked the man. 'Three-quarter Indian,' the man replied. 'And what's the other quarter?' the census-taker asked. 'My wooden leg.' "

Jack Thorpe, the son of the great Indian athlete Jim Thorpe, told me of the classic colloquy between Theodore Roosevelt and Quanah Parker, who had five wives. Mr. Roosevelt asked the Comanche chief, "Why don't you do like we do and have one wife?" Parker thought about it, "I will agree, if you will choose the one wife I should keep, and tell the other four they should go."

Many white people have had their first exposure to Indian humor through the medium of television. When Jay Silverheels, better known to millions as "Tonto," was on the Jack Paar Show, Jack inquired why Jay, a full-blooded Mohawk, had married an Italian girl. Jay ad-libbed, "I wanted to get even with Columbus."

Rodd Redwing, the Indian actor famed for his quick-draw and expert gun-handling, was getting ribbed on a TV talk show by an emcee who finally said, "Rodd, if you're so great with guns, how come in every movie you do the Indians always lose?" Rodd retorted, "Because you white men write the scripts. If we wrote them the cavalry would *never* get there in time."

Many 19th century whites liked to think of the Indian as a compulsive scalp-collector. Wit and wisdom were qualities associated with "civilization" and, therefore, not to be expected from a "savage." But, in 1892, in his *Stories from Indian Wigwams and Northern Camp Fires,* Egerton Ryerson Young translates the reply of a distinguished Indian who had been challenged to a duel by an angry white man: "I do not see any good that it would do me to put a bullet through your body. I could not make any use of you when dead, but I could of a rabbit or turkey. . . . If you want to try your pistols, take some object, say a tree or anything about my size, and if you hit that, send me word and I shall acknowledge that if I had been there you might have hit me!"

The drollery of this response is in that particular vein of dead-pan humor which European literary critics often refer to as being typically "American." Many foreigners who cite Will Rogers as a prime practitioner of this American art form are unaware of his Cherokee background.

Having listened to many rambling Indian orations, studded with improvised whimsical understatement, ironic reverse logic, and homely down-to-earth mother wit, I could not help but conclude that the typically American humor of Will Rogers was far more Cherokee in its genesis than most people would suspect. When Will Rogers said, "I don't have to make up jokes; I just tell the truth," he was describing the same kind of patient, logical, relentless *reductio ad absurdum* employed by Johnny Canoe in his article "You Great White Man" in the *Indian Time* magazine.

Here's how Johnny Canoe sees the white man's

Christmas ritual: "First, they spend money they cannot afford buying presents for other Christians whom they dislike three hundred and sixty-four days of the year. Then their squaws cook food which makes them sick. They also buy huge quantities of firewater . . . drive cars while drunk and are promptly arrested."

Then he tells the white man what the Indian thinks of paleface morality: "You form the United Nations to protect minorities, you spend a great deal of time and money discussing this, yet you neglect the Indian, who was the original ruler of the land you live in. You do research in food, and plan proper diets, yet the cost of living is so high that nobody can eat properly. You waste your national resources to such an extent that you have to appoint commissions at high salaries to look into the matter and excuse your excesses. To an innocent little Indian it is all very difficult." Johnny Canoe, like Will Rogers, isn't making up jokes, he's just telling the truth.

The initial confrontation between the Indians and the first settlers is the subject of such wry contemporary Indian observations as "First the Pilgrims landed on their knees, then they landed on us. It would have been better for us if Plymouth Rock had landed on the Pilgrims." And (a comment on the sale of Manhattan for 24 dollars worth of trinkets), "Ever since the white people moved in, our property values have been shot to hell."

In structure, if not in sentiment, these jokes are close enough to the white man's one-liners that they can be appreciated by any paleface, but there are other types of Indian humor which would not be appreciated by many whites. Some years back a white archaeologist asked Semu Huaute, the Chumash Medicine Man, if Semu knew where his grandmother was buried. Semu answered "Yes" and the archaeologist said, "I will pay you if you will take me there." Semu assured him, "You don't need to pay me. We'll make a deal. If you tell me where *your* grandmother is buried, I'll go and dig her up; and *then* I'll tell you where my grandmother is buried and you can dig her up." The archaeologist was horrified: "Dig up my grandmother? That would be sacrilegious, she's buried in holy ground."

When I relate this anecdote to Indians they roar with laughter. But I have told it to many sophisticated white people who have entirely missed the point that Semu's grandmother was also buried in holy ground and that disinterring her bones would also be sacrilegious.

Obviously there are no answers to the question "What is funny?" unless the question be re-phrased "What is considered funny in which culture under what circumstances?"

According to Hill: "The greatest contrast between Navaho and European humor lies in the degree of participation. Navaho culture possesses no system of social stratification, and because of this it is possible for every individual in the culture to participate wholly in all aspects of humorous expression. In our culture, social and educational status determine to a large extent our type of humor. Thus we find one class of society indulging predominately in a sophisticated wit involving a verbal patter with much punning, another in incredible naivete, a third in obscenity and practical joking, etc. The Navaho is under no such restrictions. Thus, it is possible for the Navaho equivalent of the European savant to indulge in a sophisticated play on words one minute and participate in some simple-minded practical joke the next without transgressing the bounds of the established cultural pattern for his humorous behavior."

Hill also describes practical jokes at the expense of those traditional comic figures—the bureaucrat and the schoolmarm: "A Navaho in the employ of the govern-

Mudheads, of clown dancers of Zuni Pueblo, New Mexico

ment was in almost daily contact with the superintendent. All business between the two was transacted through an interpreter. This continued for about six months. Finally the superintendent discovered that the man spoke almost perfect English but purposely refrained from using it as a practical joke.

"(A) school teacher . . . was very desirous of learning some Navaho songs. She finally persuaded a Navaho to teach her one. Everytime she sang the song she was greeted with gales of laughter. Finally, becoming suspicious, she had the words translated and discovered she had been taught . . . obscene verses."

Wallace reports the traditional practical joke played by the Hupa tribe on a Whilkut or Chilula visitor: "They gave him all the fatty salmon he would eat. Then he would get sick because it was too rich for him. Those people didn't have salmon where they lived and weren't used to it. After the fellow got sick, someone would offer him more salmon."

Much in the same vein is an anecdote told me by Hazel Farwell of the Tsimshian tribe. Their neighbors, the Tlingits, invited the Tsimshians to a great feast. The Tsimshians got sick because the Tlingits used seal grease. To get even with the Tlingits, the Tsimshians invited them to a great feast and served them the traditional soapberry desert—spiked with castor oil.

A retired Royal Canadian Mountie, W. J. Brummitt, reminisced in True Magazine: "I did a great deal of work with the Sarcee Indians. When I was leaving the area one old chief, whom I had arrested a number of times for drunkenness, presented me with a fancy beaded hatband. I wore it proudly and showed it to many people. Recently I ran into an old friend who was able to translate the Indian characters on the hatband for me: 'The big blue-eyed long-nosed S.O.B.' "

In some tribes, like the Hupa, practical joking is optional and there are no restrictions as to suitable targets. In other tribes practical joking is mandatory toward certain types of relatives and absolutely verboten toward other members of the family.

In *The Winnebago Tribe* Paul Radin tells us: "A man was not permitted to take even the slightest liberties with any of his near relatives or with his mother-in-law or his father-in-law, but a curious exception to this rule was permitted for his father's sister's children, his mother's brother's children, his mother's brothers, and his sisters-in-law and brothers-in-law. In the two cases last named not only was a man permitted to joke with those relatives but he was supposed to do so whenever he had an opportunity."

The "joking relationship" with a sister-in-law in a number of other tribes was described by George P. Murdock in *Our Primitive Contemporaries*. Here's what Murdock says about the Haida: "A young man . . . jokes and plays on terms of the greatest intimacy with his sister-in-law." And here's what he says about the Crow: "Between a man and his sister-in-law there prevails a relationship of excessive familiarity. They may joke together without regard to the ordinary rules of propriety. He may even raise her dress, exposing her in public, and she can retaliate in kind."

In most tribes the types of practical jokes and verbal jests which are considered appropriate for each and every kind of relative are rigidly defined. So much so, in fact, that according to John R. Swanton in his *Social Organization and Social Usages of the Indians of the Creek Confederacy*: "A Creek could tell by the attitude of any two members of his tribe toward each other—whether they joked with one another and so on—in what manner they were related . . . it was etiquette to talk disparagingly of one's own clan, even in the presence of other members of it, what was said being understood in a contrary sense. On the other hand one must always back up his father's clan and those belonging to it and must speak well of it and of them."

Armed with this Rosetta Stone, an ethnographer like Swanton could decipher both the ironic put-downs directed at one's own clan and the flattering hyperbole praising the father's clan, but the average researcher wouldn't know this. He would interpret Creek comments quite literally and the results would be somewhat less than accurate.

In *The Crow Indians* Robert H. Lowie relates the ludicrous case of the Crow who had broken the tabu and married a kinswoman from his own clan. This strange union placed the brothers of the bride in a ridiculous dilemma. Since the groom also came from their same clan he was their "brother" as well as their brother-in-law and, hence, his wife became their "sister-in-law" as well as their sister. This placed them in an impossible behavioral situation. As their sister, they were obligated to treat her with complete respect avoidance; and yet as their sister-in-law, they were obligated to engage in obscene horseplay with her.

Lowie points out an important social function of the joking-relatives: "Most significantly, the joking-relatives are a person's privileged mentors and censors when he has performed some veritably objectionable deed. In contrast to his own clan, whose function is to shield him from social obloquy, the joking-relatives deliberately try to make a man ashamed by publicly jeering him and twitting him with his improper conduct."

This inevitable reaction of the joking-relatives acts as a strong deterrent to anti-social behavior. Murdock tells us: "Ridicule serves as a powerful regulative weapon, for no punishment is more real and severe to a Crow than to be made the laughing stock of his people."

In his *Ethnography of the Fox Indians* under the heading "Control by Ridicule" William Jones relates: "In the battle . . . there was one Indian who betook himself down the bluff behind which he sought shelter

. . . where he was out of range of the bullets, and took his gun apart so that he might not have to take part in the fight. While the battle was going on the man was down there fixing his gun. Even after the battle the man was called the gunsmith, not as a term of commendation but as a term of ridicule."

Radin says: "The dislike of being made fun of, or of being the laughing stock, plays an important role among the Winnebago. It is not at all comparable to the same feeling as found at the present day among . . . people of Western Europe, for it is infinitely deeper and closely associated with social ostracism. The despondency caused by being made fun of, would frequently drive a person away from home or lead him to embark on any undertaking that would bring death."

Among the Crow such a man might become a "Crazy-Dog-Wishing-To-Die." He would then make a fetish of foolhardy bravery against the enemy. In admiration, the tribe would shower him with honors and women would bestow their favors upon him. But if, after a short time, the unhappy wretch failed to meet the death he so assiduously courted he would again become a laughing stock. The fear of losing face is every bit as strong among Indians as it is among their Asian relatives. Their hypersensitive fear of being ridiculed by whites forced them to put on that very facade of stoic dignity which so many whites wrongly construed as lack of humor.

Most whites would be astounded to learn that many tribes not only had clowns, but that in some cases they had "sacred clowns" gifted with great powers of healing. In our society it would be difficult to imagine one individual combining the functions of Red Skelton, Doctor Salk and the Archbishop of Canterbury. But that's exactly what a sacred clown had to do.

Joe Seboy, who belongs to the Sitting Bull clan of the Hunkpapa Sioux, informs me that his people call

their clowns Heyoshka and that they have two types—
"happiness" clowns and "sadness" clowns. One of Joe
Seboy's uncles is a "happiness" clown and one is a
"sadness" clown, so he is very knowledgeable about the
difference in function and modus operandi of the two
types.

Joe explains: "The Happiness Clown tries to amuse
the people. He entertains. He makes you roar with
laughter. He goes into all kinds of crazy antics. He imitates people. If there is a fat lady in the tribe, he'll
come to a dance padded way out and dressed like her.
He'll imitate the way she dances, and he'll dance like
crazy until his bloomers fall down. But the Sadness
Clown, he just wears a breechclout and paints his body.
He tries to take away your sadness. If you're sitting
there sad or lonely he'll come and sit by you. As he
looks at you, you can see him pull the sadness out of
you and take it on himself."

Unlike the situation in some other tribes, clown status in Joe's tribe is neither hereditary nor conferred. He
told me, "A boy who is meant to be a clown will know
it within himself. That power will be born within his
nature and he will start to do these things. But he must
be very careful because a clown has nature's powers.
He's a sacred man. A sadness clown is more sacred
than a happiness clown. He's more powerful than a
medicine man. He can produce rain or sunshine or anything by wishing it."

Another of my informants, who is the hereditary
clown of the Turtle Clan of the Ponca tribe, claims that
there is absolutely no religious connection to his clowning. Nevertheless, he has asked me not to reveal his
name, because the identity of the clown in his tribe is a
closely guarded secret known only to one of the subchiefs. Not even the chief knows his identity. The position is hereditary, passing from father to eldest son. If
the eldest son does not wish to assume the responsi-

bility it passes to the next son and so on. It can pass to the son of a brother or sister, but never to a sister's husband.

In some respects the function of the Ponca Clown resembles the Sioux happiness clown, in that one of his duties is to entertain at ceremonial gatherings. His identity carefully concealed in one of his disguises, usually animal skins and a mask, he sets to work. "He pulls pranks. He imitates the other dancers. The other dancers get annoyed with him because he tries to mess them up. But a good dancer can't get messed up, because he keeps his mind on what he's doing. The clown tries to throw the drummers and chanters off too if he can. But if they are any good they can't be distracted."

After the ceremonial dance is over and the participants have returned to their teepees, the Ponca Clown embarks upon another duty. It is his job "to straighten out the kids who have been bad. The parents have gone to the sub-chief, who knows who the clown is, and they have told him all the bad things their children have said and done. He tells the clown, and the clown goes and talks to them in their teepees. They call him the Booger-Man, and they are afraid of him. He knows all their faults. As he disguises himself differently each time, they don't know that he is one of their own tribe, and they are surprised he talks their language and knows all about them. He scares them, and he tells them to behave themselves or he will be back."

The "Chifonetti" or "Delight Makers" are names given by the Taos Indians to their clowns. In *Some Plays and Dances of the Taos Indians* F. M. Bailey describes the "Delight Makers" at work: "In preparation, a forty-foot pole had been brought from the mountains and set up in the plaza between the two pueblos, and a picturesque group of blanketed figures in orange, red and green stood at the foot of the pole looking up at an Indian in a red shirt, who was seated on a cross-bar

near the top arranging the prizes for which the Chifonetti were to climb the pole—a string of watermelons, a
great bag of breads with a long red streamer dangling
from it, and the whole carcass of a sheep in its wool.

The Chifonetti, with bodies and limbs fantastically
banded with black and white, their faces, with their
noses as centers, blackened in radiating lines or concen-
tric circles, and their ears decorated with bristling
bunches of corn husk, made a bizarre group. At first
they went about playing pranks on the people . . .
When tired of making sport of the onlookers, one of
the Delight Makers walked up under the pole on which
the sheep was hanging and made sheep tracks with his
fingers in the dust. Then the acting began. Another of
the band strolled by, and, discovering sheep tracks,
began trailing the animal eagerly, looking everywhere
until, glancing up, the dangling sheep caught his eye.
Then with tiny straw bows and arrows, the actors
began shooting at the sheep with great glee and horseplay. Afterwards they went through a long performance pretending to climb the pole. When the first
man slipped down, they put earth on the shaft, and
when he climbed part way up, the others dropped on
all fours, acting the part of furious bulls, pawing,
throwing up the earth, and bellowing to discourage the
climber's descent. After this they went for a short ladder and one of the group, climbing it, raised his hands
in mock dramatic manner toward the sheep and melons
beyond his reach. All sorts of clownish play and a running fire of jokes followed, but finally a long ladder was
brought and when a chain of men had reached the
upper rungs of this and then mounted on each other's
shoulders, the top man climbed a few feet and successfully reached the crossbars."

During one of the most sacred of the Navaho ceremonials, "The Night Chant," the Navaho rain god
"Water Sprinkler" is impersonated by a clown. Wash-

ington Matthews gives a description of this in *The Night Chant, A Navaho Ceremony:* "The clown . . . dances out of order and out of time. He peers foolishly at different persons. He sits on the ground, his hands clasped across his knees, and rocks his body to and fro. He joins regularly in the dance toward the close of a figure and when the others have retired he remains going through his steps, pretending to be oblivious of their departure; then, feigning to discover their absence, he follows them on a full run. He carries a fox-skin; drops it on the ground; walks away as if unconscious of its loss; pretends to become aware of his loss; acts as if searching anxiously for the skin, which lies in plain sight; screens his eyes with his hands and crouches low to look; imitates in various exaggerated ways the acts of Indian hunters; pretends at length to find the lost skin; jumps on it as if it were a live animal he was killing; shoulders it and carries it off as if it were a heavy burden; staggers and falls under it."

To a desert people like the Navaho, keeping in the good graces of their rain god would seem absolutely essential for survival. That is why it seemed strange to whites that the Navaho would let "Water Sprinkler" be portrayed as such a buffoon. White observers were even more amazed when in some of the other Navaho religious ceremonials (such as the Mountain Chant) the sacred clowns engaged very freely in farcical erotic and scatalogical activities. As Hill points out, "The inclusion of horseplay and obscenity in religious ritual is definitely untenable to most modern European thought." The key word there is *modern*.

In medieval times many Christian churches happily included obscene and scatalogical elements in their religious pageantry. From the 1823 edition (before Victorian prudery could set in) of William Hone's *Ancient Mysteries Described* we learn: "In France, at different cathedral churches, there was a Bishop or an Archbishop of Fools elected; and in the churches immediately dependent upon the papal see, a Pope of Fools. These mock pontiffs had usually a proper suite of ecclesiastics, and one of their ridiculous ceremonies was to shave the precentor of Fools upon a stage erected before the church in the presence of the populace, who were amused during the operation by his lewd and vulgar discourses accompanied by actions equally reprehensible. They were most attired in the ridiculous dresses of pantomime players and buffoons, and so habited entered the church, and performed the service accompanied by crowds of laity in masks, representing monsters, or with their faces smutted to excite fear or laughter, as occasion might require. Some of them personated females and practised wanton devices. During divine service they sung indecent songs in the choir, ate rich puddings on the corner of the altar, played at dice upon it by the side of the priest while he celebrated mass, incensed it with smoke from old burnt shoes, and ran leaping all over the church. The Bishop or Pope of Fools performed the service habited in pontifical garments, and gave his benediction; when it was concluded, he was seated in an open carriage, and drawn about to the different parts of the town followed by a large train of clergy and laymen, and a cart filled with filth, which they threw upon the populace assembled to see the procession. These licentious festivities were called the December Liberties."

In *The Golden Bough* Sir James Frazer tells us about: "The Festival of the Innocents, which was celebrated on Childermas or Holy Innocents' Day, the twenty-eighth of December. The custom was widely observed both in France and England . . . the choristers assembled in the church and chose one of their number to be a Boy Bishop, who officiated in that character with mock solemnity. Such burlesques of ecclesiastical ritual appear to have been common on that day in monasteries and convents, where the offices performed by the clergy and laity were inverted for the occasion. At the Franciscan monastery of Antibes, for example, the lay brothers, who usually worked in the kitchen and the garden, took the place of the priests on Childermas and celebrated mass in church, clad in tattered sacerdotal vestments turned inside out, holding the books upside down, wearing spectacles made of orange peel, mumbling an unintelligible jargon, and uttering frightful cries. These buffooneries were kept up certainly as late as the eighteenth century, and probably later."

Any Christian who valued his own traditions should feel right at home watching Navaho sacred ceremonies. He should understand the mystic fusion of the sublime and the ridiculous in the religious rituals of the Navaho and their neighbors the Hopi, the Pueblo, the Zuni, etc.

In *The Hopi Indians* Ruth De Ette Simpson says: "Clowns have many sacred duties whose importance is not diminished by the fact that they amuse the assembled Hopi and frequently enact nonsensical pantomimes which may become both uninhibited and crude at times."

Pueblo clowns are called "Koshare" or "Kashale." They paint their bodies with black and white stripes, with circles around the eyes and mouth. They put clay in their hair to stiffen it into one or two horns, depending on which Pueblo they live in.

In *The Standard Dictionary of Folklore, Mythology, and Legend* Gertrude Prokosch Kurath tells us: "The Koshare have the typical behavior pattern of ceremonial clowns: backward action, reverse speech, actual or simulated filth-eating, and obscenity . . . their satire on the most sacred institutions . . . and . . . their most ridiculous posturings . . . are beyond censorship."

Zuni clowns are called "Koyemshi" or "Koyemci." They are often referred to by whites as "Mudheads" because they anoint themselves from head to toe with special mud from a Sacred Lake. In *The Book of Indian Crafts and Indian Lore* Julian Harris Salomon described the "Mudheads" as follows: "They were naked except for a black kilt and black neckerchief. Their heads were covered with bag-like masks of sacking painted a brownish-pink color. These had large lumps on the top and sides of the head and doughnut-like projections around the eye and mouth openings."

Just as the folk humor of New England, New York City, and Appalachia are vastly different from one another in subject matter and in approach, the concept of clowning varies considerably from the Southwestern tribes we have been discussing to the Plains tribes. Lowie gives a fascinating account of Crow clowning in which a comic female impersonator of "Ak'bi'arusa-cari'ca" figures quite prominently: "The organizer meets his fellow-clowns in the brush, all bringing gunnysacks, mud and leaves. Of the gunnysacks they make leggings and ponchos, while the mud serves as body-paint. They make cloth masks with eye and mouth slits and blacken them with charcoal. The nose is either marked with charcoal or molded of mud and stuck on. When quite unrecognizable, the clowns leave their hiding-place and approach camp . . . The performers walk as if lame and act as clumsily as possible, so that the onlookers crowding in upon them cannot help laughing. One clown, dressed as a woman, wears a fine elk-tooth dress padded to feign pregnancy; and he must walk, talk, and sit like a woman. Another, as musician, carries a torn drum—the worst to be found . . . The clowns poke fun at every one, irrespective of his standing in the tribe . . . Before starting out, the clowns have prepared willow bows and arrows or worthless old firearms with which to frighten the people during the dance. They have also abducted the ugliest old horse, crooked-legged and swollen-kneed, and make it less attractive by tying down its ears, masking its face or plastering it with mud, and putting gunnysack leggings on its legs. The owner only discovers the theft at the performance, where it is ridden by one clown and the 'woman' behind him . . . the rider bids his companion dismount to dance. 'She' refuses, clinging to him till he gets angry and pushes her head, when she gets off and begins to perform. Her companion also prepares to dismount, but purposely tumbles down and pretends to be badly hurt. After a while he dances with his weapons, then proceeds to remount but overleaps so as to fall, when he again acts as if seriously injured. Some wags in the audience are likely to take part, asking questions and making such comments as, 'These fellows must have come from far away.' The clowns answer by gestures that they have come from a very great distance and are correspondingly fatigued . . ."

Among the Cherokee it is customary to have clowns satirize members of other races—white, black or yellow. That these exotic alter-egos open up possibilities for mischief-making not ordinarily open to the typical tabu-observing tribe member is readily apparent from this description of the Cherokee Booger or Mask Dance by Frank G. Speck and Leonard Broom in their *Cherokee Dance and Drama*s "Masked men . . . representing 'people from far away or across the water'—Germans, French, Chinese, Negroes, or even alien Indians, each wearing an appropriate mask . . . The masks representing Europeans show exaggerations of features—bushy eyebrows, moustaches, chin whiskers, red cheeks, big noses, ghastly white pallor, and bald heads. Boogers may distort their figures by stuffing abdomen, buttocks, or shins. Some carry an imitation phallus of gourd neck . . . Sometimes the gourd phallus contains water, which is released, adding to the burlesque . . . On one animated and dramatic occasion . . . when the first invader was questioned about his nationality and identity, he

199

Pablita Velarde of Santa Clara pueblo painted the
Koshare of Taos *showing the sacred clowns*
of Taos, New Mexico.

Pablita Velarde

resoundingly broke wind and this was greeted by risible applause . . . The maskers are systematically malignant. On entering, some of them act mad, fall on the floor, hit at the spectators, push the men spectators as though to get at their wives and daughters, and chase the girls toward the crowded walls . . . The host asks them what they came for and what they want. The response is decisive and candid—'Girls!' . . . The Boogers may also want 'to fight.' Both these demands are associated with Europeans, and the Indian house-party leader says they are a peaceable people and do not want to fight. Next the Booger leader says they want to dance . . . He performs awkward and grotesque steps, as if he were a clumsy white man trying to imitate Indian dancing . . . A similar dance, which lasts about five minutes, is enacted by each Booger . . . The actions of the maskers portray the Cherokee estimate of the European invader as awkward, ridiculous, lewd, and menacing."

Indian oral literature is particularly rich in humor. There are whole cycles of comic etiological legends giving hilarious explanations of natural phenomena or the peculiar characteristics of living creatures. Typical examples are: "Why the 'Possum's Tail is Bony" (Biloxi), "Why 'Possum has a Big Mouth" (Choctaw), and "How Coyote Created Man" (Nez Perce).

"Coyote" is an enigma to many white scholars. To Indians "Coyote" is at one and the same time beneficent Creator, conniving trickster and bungling idiot. He's Jehovah, Sergeant Bilko and Jerry Lewis rolled into one.

This ubiquitous comic character with the three-way schizophrenic split appears in different forms in the tales told by different tribes. In addition to Coyote, the Trickster also appears as Hare, Raven, Mink, Blue Jay and as Old Man, White Man and Whiskey Jack.

To the white man's eye many Trickster tales don't

seem very funny. But they weren't designed for the white man's eye but for the red man's ear. As Hill points out: "The success of the humor is . . . dependent upon the storyteller's ability as a raconteur . . . pantomiming . . . the actions and mimicking . . . the voices of the animal characters."

Trickster, of course, resolved nothing, except in so far as he demonstrated what happens when man's instinctual side is given free reign. He is the symbol for that instinctual side and, overtly, as we have just seen, he can serve either as an object lesson or made to be ridiculous, and become a source of laughter and amusement. If we follow instincts, so runs the ethical, philosophical meaning of the myth, we lose our sense of proportion and we kill others as well as ourselves.

But Trickster is not merely the symbol for the instinctual. He is likewise the symbol for the irrational and the non-socialized. For the Winnebago, for all primitive peoples, in fact, they all belonged together. They dreaded all three and tried to create as many safeguards against them as possible. Yet they recognized only too well that man could relapse into all three at a moment's notice. Every man, they felt, possessed a Trickster unconscious which it was imperative for both the individual concerned and, even more so, for society, to bring to consciousness lest it destroy him and those around him."

Linguistic elements are important in Indian humor. Hill tells us: "The great number of homonymous elements in Navaho, due largely to the leveling influence of phonetic laws . . . make Navaho a peculiarly tempting language for the punster."

And Lowie says: "Verbal cleverness is common among the Crow and they play with words as such." He gives several examples of Crow puns where the primary meaning is a person's given name and the secondary meaning is a literal interpretation of the words comprising the name.

Then there's the question of pronunciation. In *The Humor of Primitive Peoples* Henry A. Bowman informs us: "It seems very humorous to a Kootenay . . . when a white man, struggling to master the difficult native gutturals, pronounces the word for 'rainbow' like the word for 'horsefly', and says 'owl' instead of 'woodpecker', and 'skunk' instead of 'crow'."

This is only the other side of the coin from our teasing a Japanese who can't tell the difference between an "election" and an "erection."

Indian wits are great simile coiners. Lowie quotes a Crow wit, Grey-Bull, who defended polygamy and promiscuity thusly: "Women are like a herd of buffalo, and a husband who cleaves to one wife is like a hunter who has killed the last of the fugitive animals and stays by the carcass because he lacks spirit to pursue others."

Indian orators also know their way around a metaphor. When a bureaucrat from the detested Bureau of Indian Affairs pontificated, "We must bring the Indians up to our cultural level," Mad Bear corrected him: "You mean down to your level. You want us to get out of our safe canoe and into your sinking battleship."

Bruce Grant cites two famous 19th century comic metaphors in *American Indians, Yesterday and Today:* "A Wichita chief, after listening to the arguments of some white commissioners, reached down and took up a handful of dust and threw it into the air. As it blew away in thousands of particles, he said: 'There are as many ways to cheat the Indians.'

"Red Bear, a Sioux chief said: 'When the Great Father sent out men to our people, I was poor and thin; now I am large and stout and fat. It is because I have been stuffed full of lies.' "

Modern Indians also create their own slang. Young bucks refer to amorous visitations as "teepee creeping." Those Indians who try to curry favor with the Bureau of Indian Affairs are called "Uncle Tom Toms."

Indians also have a rich store of humorous proverbs. The great Chief Joseph of the Nez Perce was quoted by *The New York Sun* as having used these: Look twice at a two-faced man; Cursed be the hand that scalps the reputation of the dead; The eye tells what the tongue would hide; Fire-water courage ends in trembling fear; Big name often stands on small legs, and finest fur may cover toughest meat.

In 1906 *The Boston Herald* reprinted these Indian proverbs collected in that part of Oklahoma which was then the Indian Territory:

There are three things it takes a strong man to hold—a young warrior, a wild horse, and a handsome squaw;

No Indian ever sold his daughter for a name;

Before the paleface came there was no poison in the Indian's corn;

When a fox walks lame, old rabbit jumps;

The paleface's arm is no longer than his word;

A squaw's tongue runs faster than the wind's legs;

There is nothing so eloquent as a rattlesnake's tail;

If the Indian would lie like the paleface, he would rule the earth;

The Indian scalps his enemy; the paleface skins his friends;

The Indian takes his dog to heaven; the paleface sends his brother to hell;

There will be hungry palefaces as long as there is any Indian land to swallow.

Other Indian proverbs not overly flattering to the Paleface include:

White man build one fire—freeze face and burn backside. Indian build two fires and stand between;

White man cheat Indian once, white man's fault.
White man cheat Indian twice, Indian's fault.

Here are a few moral maxims: May I walk in another man's moccasins for two weeks before I pass judgment on him (Sioux); A man must make his own arrows (Omaha); and, All strangers are potentially gods in disguise, honor them as such—until they prove that they are not.

And as a final benediction, here is some good practical advise: Don't use up all your kindling to get the fire started; Color don't count if the colt don't trot (Cherokee); Even a hawk is an eagle among crows (Apache); Speak not loudly to each other unless the teepee is on fire (Ojibwa advice to the newly wed); Do not use a tomahawk to remove a fly from your friend's forehead.

TECUMSEH

by Walter Jarrett

*I*f the present day advocates of Red Power and Pan-Indianism need an idol they need search no farther than the great Shawnee Chief Tecumseh. Realizing that the contact of white and Indian civilizations always meant the eventual supremacy of the white, with the decay and destruction of the Indian, Tecumseh attempted to block the white advance into the old Northwest Territory by forming a federation of Indian tribes that reached all the way from Alabama to Minnesota and from Kansas to New England—and almost succeeded.

Born in Ohio in the spring of 1768, Tecumseh was the son of the Shawnee chief Pucksinwah, head of the Kispokotha sept, or clan. His mother was named Methotasa (early writers incorrectly referred to her as a Creek or Cherokee) and at the time of Tecumseh's birth his parents were on their way to an important council at Chillicothe, located at the present site of Oldtown, Greene County, Ohio, three miles north of the county seat, Xenia. For five years the various septs of the Shawnees had been meeting at Chillicothe at intervals in an effort to determine what the Shawnees should do, as a nation, about the whites who, despite treaties forbidding it, were crossing the mountains to the east and spilling into lands used by that tribe.

When Tecumseh was six years of age his father was killed by a white hunting party. Thereafter the young boy was guided and trained by his older brother, Chiksika. He was taught Shawnee history, traditions and codes of the tribe. As was the custom, Tecumseh had to commit these matters to perfect memory and learn to repeat them verbatim with nothing added, altered or omitted. From his mother and older sister, Tecumapese, the young Indian learned the value of patience and the need for pity for those without power, and that cruelty for the sake of cruelty, whether to animals or man, degraded a person. By the time he was eight years old Tecumseh was already exhibiting signs of leadership. By this time the Americans were already establishing settlements in the traditional hunting grounds of the Shawnee—Can-tuc-Kee (Kentucky)—and the Shawnee, like other tribes of the old Northwest, increasingly realized that their total elimination was not far distant if they did not fight back. The ever-increasing number of whites were driving off the game and taking possession of the land. Far away in Washington, the government of the whites continued to give lip service to the fiction of Indian independence and land ownership, but the Indian was more impressed by the rapidity with which the whites obtained any area they coveted. No opposition short of war seemed to have the least chance of damming the white flood. And in the spring of 1777 the Shawnees, under the leadership of Tecumseh's godfather, Black Fish, went to war against the settlers of Kentucky. It was to be a war without end for the Shawnees, who were supported by the British, who desired to retain the lucrative Great Lakes fur trade and were glad to help the Indians keep the aggressive American frontiersmen as far as possible from Canada. The Indians preferred trading with the British to trading with the Americans and felt no danger from Canadian expansion.

As the Shawnee war waged on year after year, other tribes occasionally joined them in battle against the Americans. The Indians, even those who had been friendly toward the whites in the beginning, were becoming increasingly resentful of the way in which they suffered at the hands of the white men. They were cheated at trading posts after being plied with whiskey until their reasoning powers were gone. An Indian might trade a year's catch of furs for a few trinkets and a little bad whiskey. He gave the trinkets to his wife, drank the whiskey and was left with nothing but a heavy head to show for a year's work. Too, the white man's diseases wreaked havoc among the Indians with whom they came into contact along the advancing frontier. Such was the world in which Tecumseh grew up.

In the spring of 1779 the situation grew so bad for the Shawnees that the nation split up and hundreds of men, women and children left the homeland in Ohio and moved across the Mississippi, hoping to find a new home—and relief from the constant war. But Black Fish, Chiksika, and the white chief, Blue Jacket, remained behind. Of course, Tecumseh and the rest of his family stayed in Ohio with his brother, Chiksika.

In the spring of 1783 Tecumseh took part in his first battle against the whites and, at the age of fifteen, outshone even the ablest warriors of the Shawnee. He killed four men in the fight and helped Chiksika kill another. The most any other Shawnee killed in the battle was two. One white was taken prisoner. Later, at the Shawnee camp he was burned alive. Tecumseh found the torture and burning of the prisoner so revolting that, without any voice in tribal matters as of yet, he protested. In an impassioned speech he pointed out that such cruelty was unworthy of real men, of Shawnees, and swore that never again would he take part in the torture of any living creature, man or animal, nor would he consider as friend any man who allowed himself to take part in anything so degrading. The vigorous manner and eloquence with which he spoke so impressed his companions that they agreed with him not to repeat the act. Tecumseh never altered his resolution. Time and again he protected women and children from his infuriated followers. Years later, at the battle of Fort Meigs, a party of Americans were captured by the British and Indians. Although the Americans had surrendered as prisoners of war, they were herded into an outdoor pen and the British general, Henry A. Procter, gave the Indians leave to select any man among the prisoners and kill him in any manner desired. The Indians were firing point blank into the huddled Americans, others were being selected and tomahawked in cold blood when Tecumseh arrived on the scene. Slamming to a halt, leaping from his mount and brandishing his war club, he rushed to the aid of an American, Colonel John Dudley. Two Indians had grabbed him, one had jerked his head back by the hair and the other was just about to stab him. Tecumseh knocked the knife-wielder aside and ordered the other to turn the prisoner loose. Instead the Indian whipped out his knife and cut Dudley's throat, severing the jugular vein. Tecumseh struck the Indian a blow on the head with his club, killing him. Tecumseh then ordered the other Indians to stop the slaughter, which they did, then addressed them scathingly, calling them cowards and saying that he would slay anyone who harmed another prisoner. Turning to Procter, he asked, "Why have you allowed this massacre?"

"Sir," replied Procter, "your Indians cannot be commanded."

"Begone," was the angry reply of the outraged Tecumseh. "You are unfit to command. Go, put on petticoats."

Tecumseh put the remaining prisoners under the guard of four warriors, warning them that if any more were killed or abused, all four would be executed. He then ordered the others to mount up and follow him back to the battle where brave men, not cowards, were needed.

When Chiksika was killed in battle in April, 1788, there was no question of Tecumseh's taking over the command of the remaining Kispokotha Shawnees, who were then fighting against the whites with the Cherokees. The accession was so automatic that no vote had to be taken. Time and time again the young Tecumseh led his band to victory. He was possessed with an uncanny knack of assessing any situation in an instant and acting immediately in a manner which at once swung the scales in his favor. The Shawnees realized that no one else approached his qualifications for leadership.

Tecumseh watched the advance of the whites and the progressive deterioration of the Indians with an evergrowing surge of anger. He was certain in his own mind that the land belonged to the Indian tribes forever, no matter by what show of legality it might be taken away from them, and that they could cling to their culture and traditions. From the east the tide of whites was ever-increasing, moving toward the lands west of the Ohio river and filling up the Kentucky hunting grounds where the once great herds of buffalo were now becoming scarce. It is not known when the idea of banding the Indians into a vast confederation to drive the white invaders back again beyond the Ohio and the mountains occurred to Tecumseh. But he was still a young man when he concluded that the only possible method of opposing the white advance successfully was to obtain the cooperation of all the Indians and to have them act in concert.

By 1795 Tecumseh found himself with a large number of followers. Tall, handsome and modest, he refrained from boasting of his own prowess, being content to let others boast of him and let his actions speak for themselves. It was in the spring of that year that Tecumseh moved the members of his sept to the banks of Deer Creek in the vicinity of present London, Ohio, and several hundred members of other septs, most of whom were young men, followed him, seeing in Tecumseh the makings of a great new chief. Everything the young chief did turned out well—with two exceptions. One was allowing his younger brother, Lowawluwaysica—who would become known as the Prophet— to assume second in command of his following. Where Tecumseh was tall and perfectly proportioned, his brother was a head shorter and ugly; where Tecumseh was gentle and good-natured, Lowawluwaysica was devious and surly—and would eventually destroy his brother's plans of an Indian confederation.

Tecumseh's second mistake was marrying the Peckuwe maiden, Monetohse. While she was slender and attractive, she was also demanding and found fault in everything her husband did. While Tecumseh was able to overlook her behavior toward himself, he could not overlook the fact that she neglected to care for his son, born two years after the marriage. He invoked an ancient Shawnee marital law and dissolved their marriage, sending Monetohse back to her parents in disgrace, and placed his son in charge of his older sister, Tecumapese.

Tecumseh refused to have any part of the peace

treaty signed between the whites and representatives of various Indian tribes at Fort Greenville in August, 1795. The treaty gave the whites twenty-five thousand square miles of Indian territory as well as sixteen tracts *within* lands left to the Indians for government reservations. Representatives of the twelve tribes who attended the treaty conference were given $1,666 for each tribe, and promised an annual allowance of $825! As far as Tecumseh was concerned it was out and out thievery of Indian lands and any agreement with the whites was worthless. Upon being told of the terms of the agreement by the white Shawnee chief, Blue Jacket, Tecumseh said: "My heart is a stone: heavy with sadness for my people; cold with the knowledge that no treaty will keep whites out of our lands; hard with the determination to resist as long as I live and breathe. Now we are weak and many of our people are afraid. But hear me; a single twig breaks, but the bundle of twigs is strong. Someday I will embrace our brother tribes and draw them into a bundle and together we will win our country back from the whites."

The Treaty of Greenville brought peace to the Ohio land and the real white settlement of Ohio by whites began in earnest. William Henry Harrison was given command of Fort Washington and charged with protecting the new white settlers as the Shawnee land became checkered with new farms.

A short time after the signing of the Greenville Treaty Tecumseh took a new wife, an older woman named Mamate. Mamate gave birth to a son in the summer of 1796 and died soon afterwards. The new baby was named Nay-tha-way-nah and given to Tecumapese to care for. Perhaps the birth of his second son reminded Tecumseh that the place of his own birth was already the site of a white farm. He became determined to win back the land that rightfully belonged to the Shawnees. Too, the plan of an Indian confederation was never far from his mind and the way to such a confederation was shown to him when the Delawares, who had been pushed out of lands given to them by treaty time and time again, came to him in 1798. The Delawares had heard much of the young Shawnee chief who was so strong in all ways. Would Tecumseh come and bring his Shawnees to live with the Delawares and lead them too? Tecumseh led his followers into Indiana territory to join the Delawares. Within a year other Ohio tribes had come under Tecumseh's sphere of influence, impressed not only with his reputation for fairness and proven ability to lead men, but also the eloquence with which he held audiences spellbound.

Soon after joining the Delawares, Tecumseh began traveling and addressing councils of various Indian tribes in an effort to bring them into what he saw as a powerful amalgamation of Indian strength and power. He traveled to the council fires of what remained of the Iroquois Confederation in the east; nearer home he spoke to the Wyandots, the Potawatomies and others. The Hurons, Ottawas and Chippewas, Winnebagos, Foxes, Sacs, Menominees of Michigan, Wisconsin and Canada would hear him, as would the Sioux, Mandans and Cheyennes west of the Mississippi; in the south the Natchez and Choctaws of Mississippi, traditional enemies, sat down together in council with him, as did the Creeks, the Seminoles, Chickasaws, Alabamas, the Biloxis and his old friends, the Cherokees. He urged the Indians to prohibit the consumption of any alcoholic beverage and the smoking of marijuana, to study closely and seriously the ways of the whites and to break all alliances with them, and to take no part in the white man's fight with other whites.

Too, he encouraged the Indians to appear weak, to swallow their pride and fall back, and under no pretext take up arms against the whites until the time was ready, the time when all Indians would take up the fight together. For that fight, Tecumseh told them he would give the sign. It would be a sign that would come to all the tribes on the same day and at the same time. Tecumseh hoped that when the time came the whites would vacate the Indian lands west of the mountains peacefully but if they would not then the great wave of Indians from all tribes, fighting together, would sweep across the land and destroy the whites to the last man.

Meanwhile William Henry Harrison had pulled political strings to have himself appointed governor of Indiana. He arrived at his new post in early 1801 and soon began new land acquisitions by negotiations with the Indians. In 1802-1803 another million acres were added to lands available for white settlement. Other treaties followed, and the resulting Indian resentment was attributed by Harrison to British influence. Harrison had little sympathy for the Indians and was convinced that the only possible way to deal satisfactorily with them was to destroy them. He had visions of himself as a great conquerer of Indian lands and mapped out grandiose campaigns and felt that all he needed was an opportunity to exhibit his abilities as a strategist. He was not yet aware of Tecumseh, but Tecumseh was very aware of William Henry Harrison.

Tecumseh continued to travel, recruiting tribe after tribe to join his confederation and give their aid when the great sign was given. When he spoke of the great sign he never failed to awe his audience. When the period of waiting was over, he told them, and tribal unification had been completed, he would stamp his foot and the earth would tremble and roar. He promised that great trees would fall, streams would change their courses and run backwards, and lakes would be swallowed up into the earth and elsewhere new lakes would appear. The sign would shake men everywhere to their very bones like nothing they had ever known before. But when it came they were told to drop their hunting bows, their hoes, leaving their fields and camps and assemble across the lake from the fort of Detroit. On that day tribes would cease to exist. They would all be Indians, one people united forever for the good of all!

In the summer of 1802 Tecumseh preached his message across the northeast, in Vermont and Massachusetts, two years later he was in Minnesota talking to the Sioux. Everywhere he went he carried the same message and when he left it was with the assurance that another tribe would join him when the time came. In 1805 Tecumseh and Lowawluwaysica, who now called himself the Shawnee Prophet, established a new village near Fort Greenville that was not a Shawnee village but an *Indian* village where all Indians, regardless of tribe, were welcome. A year later William Henry Harrison became aware of Tecumseh's activities and wrote a letter to the Delawares in which he accused them of pursuing a "dark, thorny" path by following the "pretended prophet" and asked them to call upon the Shawnee Prophet and demand that he show some sign of his powers. A party of forty Delawares did call upon the Prophet, who, frightened, turned to Tecumseh and asked what he must do. Tecumseh pointed out that he could foretell what would happen just as their brother Chiksika and their father Pucksinwah had been able to do. The fact that Tecumseh was the true prophet was known only to himself and his brother. Tecumseh allowed everyone else to think that his younger brother could foretell the future. Tecumseh instructed his brother to tell the Delawares that fifty days from that day the sky would turn black at high noon, the night creatures would stir and the stars would shine. The Shawnee Prophet did as he was told and, of course, was credited with predicting the eclipse. Unfortunately the Shawnee Prophet forgot that his brother was the true prophet as he enjoyed his newfound fame.

Meanwhile Tecumseh became friends with a family of whites named Galloway and one of his greatest joys was discussing at length matters of politics, religion, ethics and such with James Galloway. Galloway had a fine library with which the Indian chief acquainted himself; *Hamlet* becoming his favorite tale. Tecumseh could speak English quite well but while he could read and write the whiteman's language, he was not fluent enough to read the more difficult books in the Galloway library. James Galloway's fourteen year old daughter, Rebecca, offered to help him. She spent many hours teaching the Shawnee chief who was now thirty-eight years of age. In the spring of 1808, when she turned seventeen Tecumseh asked for Rebecca's hand in marriage. Rebecca thought over the marriage proposal for a month and then agreed to marry Tecumseh, with whom she was in love, but only if he would adopt her people's mode of life and dress. He thought over her request for a month, then returned and told her that to do as she wanted would lose him the respect and leadership of his people. Rebecca Galloway wept when Tecumseh took leave of her for the last time.

That same year Tecumseh had his first interview with William Henry Harrison. He promised Harrison peace if the United States did not make further treaties involving land cessions and added that if such cessions were made, he would form an alliance with the English and make war on the Americans. Harrison dismissed Tecumseh's request as preposterous. A year later the two men met again but by this time events made peace impossible. Illinois Territory was created, leaving Indiana with its present boundaries. Harrison received permission from the secretary of war to buy more Indian land; the purchase of 2,500,000 acres in the fall of 1809 increased the number and wrath of Indians hostile to the United States. While Tecumseh maintained

Tecumseh defending the white prisoners at Fort Meigs

that the Indians held the land in common, that no one tribe owned this or that territory, Harrison couldn't agree with him less and pointed out that had the Great Spirit intended to make one nation of the Indians, he would not have put different languages into their heads, but would have taught them all to speak alike. Tecumseh replied bitterly that no one tribe had the right to give away or sell what belonged to all and not until the United States agreed to cease purchasing lands from Indians and restored the lands recently bought, would peace be possible. Pointing to the moon that had risen on the council, Governor Harrison said that the moon would sooner fall to the earth than the United States would give up the lands. "Then," said Tecumseh, "I suppose that you and I will have to fight it out."

Another council was held in August, 1810 between Tecumseh and Harrison that was just as fruitless. Describing the arrival of Tecumseh at the conference, Captain George R. Floyd, commanding officer of Fort Knox, wrote: ". . . they were headed by the brother of the Prophet, Tecumseh, who perhaps is one of the finest looking men I ever saw—about six feet high, straight, with large, fine features, and altogether a daring, bold looking fellow."

The next day this "daring, bold looking fellow" let Harrison know for the last time that he meant business. The meeting got started on a bad note when Harrison told Tecumseh that "Your father wishes you to take a chair." The very idea of the governor calling himself "your father" was repugnant to Tecumseh.

Tecumseh spoke first and pointed out that he felt that the Americans were trying to force the red people to do some injury to the whites so the latter would have an excuse to war on the Indians and that they were "continually driving the red people; when, at last, you will drive them into the Great Lake, where they can't either stand or walk." The Shawnee chief ended with a threat: "We shall have a great council, at which all the tribes will be present, when we shall show to those who sold that they had no right to the claim that they set up; and we will see what will be done to those chiefs that did sell the land to you. I am not alone in this determination; it is the determination of all the warriors and red people who listen to me. I now wish *you* to listen to me. If you do not, it will appear as if you wished me to kill all the chiefs that sold you the land. I tell you so because I am authorized by all the tribes to do so. I am the head of them all! I am a warrior and all the warriors will meet together in two or three moons from this. Then I will call for those chiefs that sold you the land and shall know what to do with them. If you do not restore the land, you will have a hand in killing them."

As for confidence in yet another treaty with the whites, Tecumseh asked: "How can we have confidence in the white people? When Jesus Christ came on earth, you killed him and nailed him to a cross . . ."

Harrison's reply was as highhanded as ever and caused the followers of Tecumseh to bring out their arms. They were stilled by the chief and left the council. Another council in July of the next year ended much the same way.

Autumn of 1811 found Tecumseh in the south addressing councils of Cherokees, Seminoles, Choctaws and Chickasaws; autumn of 1811 found William Henry Harrison planning to attack Tecumseh's Tippecanoe village in his absence. Harrison gathered 1000 men, mostly volunteers, and with a well-planned campaign already formulated, prepared to annihilate his unsuspecting enemies—an act that he forgot to report to the president. He left Vincennes on September 26, 1811, and moved directly up the Wabash, paused long enough to build Fort Harrison on the present site of

Terre Haute, and on the night of November 6, encamped on Tippecanoe Creek. Before leaving Tecumseh had warned his followers, and especially his brother, the Shawnee Prophet, to avoid battle with the whites at all costs. At long last he could see the fulfillment of his years of work: the Indian confederation now actually existed and the time for war was almost at hand.

That night the Prophet sent a deputation of three men to Harrison and it was settled that the terms of peace were to be arranged the next day. But the next morning, under orders from the Prophet, who told them that not only would they be victorious but that he had rendered the bullets of the white men to be harmless when fired against them, the Indians treacherously attacked the Americans. The conflict was fierce and bloody with the Indians rushing boldly and openly to clinch with the enemy. The Prophet perched himself on a hill nearby and chanted a war song—but not for long. When messengers raced to him to say that the Indians were dying in a most natural way, he urged them on, then deserted them. When the warriors saw that the fire of the whites was just as lethal as ever and that the Prophet had fled, they became demoralized and retreated. The white casualties were 61 killed and 127 wounded; the Indian losses were unknown. Harrison immediately dispatched messengers to the East with reports of an overwhelming defeat of the Indians. In later years there was much controversy as to whether or not Harrison had actually won. He had avoided rout and repulsed the Indians but he also found it necessary to retreat almost immediately. But the fact that the Indians had fought and had not won an overwhelming victory all but ruined Tecumseh and dashed the Indian confederation on the very eve of its birth.

Tecumseh arrived back at Tippecanoe only four days after the fateful battle, his face as frozen as stone.

Shaking his brother, fallen and disgraced, by the hair until his nose began to bleed, he told him that death was too good, too easy, for him. In a day he had destroyed what it had taken Tecumseh a decade to build. The Prophet was drummed out of the camp. He was no longer an Indian, he no longer existed.

As Tecumseh had predicted, the earth did shake. On December 16, 1811, a deep, terrifying rumble was felt in the south of Canada. Trees fell and huge trees toppled. Lake Michigan and Lake Erie trembled and great waves broke on the shores, though the day was windless. In the west the earth shuddered so fiercely that great heards of bison staggered to their feet and stampeded, and in the south whole forests fell. In Missouri the town of New Madrid was destroyed, the Mississippi river turned and flowed backwards. The earthquake lasted for two days and filled the atmosphere with choking dust. A second struck on January 23, and a third hit four days later. The fourth and worst quake came on February 13, and lasted for an hour. It did more damage than the other three combined. Many of those that had deserted Tecumseh's cause reconsidered for this was very strong medicine but it was too late. The defeat at Tippecanoe had taken the ardor for war out of too many of his followers.

Those that remained faithful followed Tecumseh into the British service in the War of 1812, which broke out immediately. But Tecumseh, commissioned as a major-general, was doomed to continued disaster. The English commander, General Henry Procter, was incompetent and, in all the qualities of real manhood, the inferior of his Indian ally. After the battle of Put-in-Bay, on Lake Erie, he started to retreat. Tecumseh protested and was induced to go on only by the promise that winter supplies would be delivered a few miles up the Thames. It was on this stream that Procter finally determined to make a stand, but at the onset of the action he retreated with his red coats, leaving the Indians to bear the brunt of the battle, Tecumseh was killed. Only one person at the site of the battle could identify the Shawnee chief and that was the Kentucky frontiersman, Simon Kenton. While at least four Americans claimed the honor of having killed Tecumseh, as far as is known Kenton never identified his body.

But there on the banks of a quiet Canadian stream, thirty-five miles from Detroit, the great Tecumseh, statesman, diplomat, a man devoted to the cause of his people and yet a humble and modest intellectual, found an unmarked grave. The Indians lost their greatest leader, the whites won the Northwest.

IS GERONIMO ALIVE AND WELL IN THE SOUTH VIETNAMESE CENTRAL HIGHLANDS?

by Don Dedera

A more terror-stricken class of people than the citizens of these territories I have never found. One hundred forty have been murdered.

"(The enemy) roams 600 miles to the north and south, and 400 miles to the east and west."

The communique could be from any one of several troubled corners of the world today. Rather, it was from the commander of the military department of Arizona 85 years ago.

Brigadier General Nelson A. Miles was attempting to explain to his president how fewer than 200 guerrillas could run riot in a land under protection of more than half of all the combat troops of the United States Army.

So classically successful were the Apaches, the Arizona border campaigns deserve study by modern anti-insurgents. The hard lessons of the Sulphur Springs Valley bear currently upon the situation in the Middle East and, to some extent, the increasing terrorism in American cities. In short, it is as though Geronimo has been reincarnated as a Viet Cong general.

Political circumstances are dissimilar, of course, but many military aspects are comparable. The Apaches would not reconcile themselves to white domination. They retarded settlement of a vast wilderness—larger than Germany and France combined. They were the last American Indians in substantial numbers to resist; a nation of five thousand versus fifty million. Never had the guerrilla advantage been exploited more effectively.

As late as 1861, a newspaper concluded that, "Nineteen-twentieths of the entire territory of Arizona is under the undisputed control of the Apache." At the same time General William T. Sherman was saying, "The best advice I can offer is to notify the settlers to withdraw, and then to withdraw the troops and leave the country to the aboriginal inhabitants."

The Sioux won battles but lost wars. The Apaches lost at the battles of Apache Pass, Big Dry Wash and Skeleton Cave, deduced that frontal challenge was suicide and adapted to avoid defeat.

A junior officer in the frontier campaigns said flatly, "The Apache was unlike any other Indian tribe the whites have ever fought. . . . His mode of warfare was peculiarly his own. He saw no reason for fighting unless there was something tangible and immediate to be gained. . . . His creed was 'fight and run away, live to fight another day.' "

Central to Apache strength, they were at home in a revered land they had every reason to call their own. Long ago their Athapascan forefathers had migrated from the Arctic Circle to the Sonoran Desert. By test of arms they had won their territory.

Geronimo

"No Indian had more virtues and none has been more truly ferocious when aroused," in the opinion of the Indian fighter, Captain John G. Bourke. "He (the Apache) was the first of the native Americans to defeat in battle or outwit in diplomacy the all-conquering, smooth-tongued Spaniard." By the time Anglo-Americans arrived in force, the Apaches were the greatest negative human force from West Texas to Central Arizona, from Colorado to Chihuahua. Pacification was complicated by four overlapping military commands within five political subdivisions of two mutually suspicious countries.

Apaches knew every copse and gulch of their broken, varied range. They were tough, resourceful, elemental. They were as at home on the desert floor as in the "steepest, highest, rockiest mountains where one would not believe a bird would dare to fly."

Their long-time foe, General George Crook, described them, "As little like the well-fed Indian of the eastern reservation as the hungry wolf to the sleek house dog." And again, "Tigers of the human species."

In a rite of manliness, Apache youths were made to swim in ice-choked streams, and melt snowballs in their armpits. At seven they received their first weapons. Bands of Apache boys played war by shooting arrows into wasp nests, expecting to be stung. "Make us brave," they begged of the wasps. And always there was the running; with a mouthful of water to encourage breath control; with a heavy stone in each fist to hone endurance.

Chatto told his son, "You know no one will help you in this world. You must do something. You will run to the top of the mountain and come back. That will make you strong. My son, you know no one is your friend, not even your sister, father or mother. Your leg is your friend; your brain is your friend; your sight is your friend."

Apache braves could make ninety miles afoot in thirteen hours. On the side of a hill, they could out-run a horse. They could scamper through fields of cactus that would halt cavalry. Nor were the males the only dauntless travelers of the race. An Apache squaw was captured by Mexicans in Sonora and sold into slavery in Baja California. She escaped and walked home—a thousand miles up the Baja Peninsula, across California and Arizona, through a dozen enemy nations, without provisions, weapons or maps.

Lieutenant Britton Davis documented the grit of an eighteen year old Chihuahua Apache maiden, wounded in the thigh a year before he saw her. "It had remained a running sore, and the limb below it had shriveled to mere bone and skin, as immovable as a rod of iron. Yet she had ridden and walked hundreds of miles with her people in their many changes of camps in Mexico, and rode the 300 miles from near Nacori, Sonora, to San Carlos (Ariz.) with them on this trip out with the general. She was hardly more than skin and bones herself but we had a hard time persuading her to let our surgeons amputate the limb; an amputation that restored her to health."

White men have written (with characteristic ethnocentrism) of Apache bands "encumbered by women and children." Another point of view was expressed by Jason Betzinev, who fought with Geronimo: "Right in the thick of the fighting one old Apache woman volunteered to go out for a sack of 500 cartridges which some exhausted runner had dropped while fleeing. The old woman successfully brought in that bag of ammunition just as the men were running short. Not all heroes are warriors!"

Such women bore and nurtured a kind of warrior; courageous, adept and disciplined. One brave is known to have been wounded eight times, yet he fought on. With only loincloths they could endure severe temperature changes. They were unequaled at tracking and reading trail signs. Messages of considerable detail could be transmitted to friends by trailside arrangements of stones and sticks. By smoke and fireflashes, intelligence could be sent 100 miles in an hour. Their camouflage was magical. Knee-length moccasins protected them from snakes and spines. They had an instinct for psychological warfare.

Historian Dr. Ralph H. Ogle wrote, "The Apaches' idea of war was to keep a general feeling of insecurity for life and property among their victims, striking them only when there could be no retaliation. Effective communication allowed small detached bands to operate in unusual concert and to maintain control over the vast region they inhabited."

Also of note, warring Apaches could count on support of native populations; could recruit or impress reinforcements; could find refuge close to the enemy. Tribal loyalties were tied to extremes of bestiality and compassion, torture for the vanquished, plunder for the victorious. Around the council fires the sins of the white man were smoked into Apache lore. Apache excesses were justified by a litany that ever began: The whites were foreign invaders of the motherland.

As often as not, when regular troops did manage to overtake an Apache war party, the stiff procedures of command schools were dutifully followed: "Left into line!" "Dismount!" "Count fours!" "Numbers four—hold horses!" "Numbers one, two and three—ten paces to the front."

And while the cavalry was going by the book, the Apaches were vanishing into the mountains. Even when fortune turned against them, the Apaches drew upon their raw genius for survival. Seldom has the American cavalry been so humiliated as it was by Victorio. With never more than 300 men he raided at will amidst two armies—once stealing fifty horses and dismounting the American cavalry post at Ojo Caliente. Totally frustrated by Victorio, Lieutenant G. W. Smith lashed out at civilian critics, "If you will come down here, I will give you a sample Cavalry ride on a trail toward Old Mexico, which, long before it (the ride) is ended, will convince you that talk is one thing and work is another. . . ."

In November, 1879, fifteen heavily-armed vigilantes from the Mexican hamlet of Carrizal were ambushed and wiped out. Victorio calmly waited for the rescue party and slaughtered it, too, to the last man. "Tacticians compare his campaigns to the most skillful military movements of all time. How did he do it? The answer lies in the desert which bred those indestructible warriors. A hundred miles in the saddle was just a good ride for them. A couple of days without water was merely part of the task. A meal of mesquite beans would keep them going until something better turned up.

"The whole difference between them and their pursuers is summed up in one detail," wrote C. L. Sonnichsen. "When Col. Buell went into Mexico on Victorio's track, he cast proud glances at a 400-gallon water wagon which he had invented himself. The Indians, if they carried anything to drink at all, transported it in a 30-foot length of horse intestines, casually cleaned out, filled with drinkable (by their standards) fluid, and wrapped around the neck and body of a pack horse. The did not have much, but they used what they had with incomparable efficiency."

Then there was seventy-three year old Nana, who despite his infirmities led a thousand-mile, two-month raid into the United States in July, 1881. His forty braves killed forty whites and wounded many more. Nana won eight sharp fights, most with American troops. He captured two enemy and 200 remounts. Eluding 1,400 troops and armed civilians, he retreated

Geronimo (at left) and Natchez mounted.
Geronimo's son stands at his side holding his grandson.

to his Mexican sanctuary without any loss of personnel.

Two years later Chatto and Benito with twenty-six warriors raided for six days across 400 miles without once being seen by a soldier. They lost one man. Except for naps on horseback, Chatto went sleepless the entire raid. "The worst band of Indians in America," General George Crook called them.

But in November, 1885, Josanie outdid Chatto. Josanie with ten comrades in one month traveled 1200 miles, wore out 250 horses, murdered thirty-eight people, and although dismounted twice, escaped to Mexico. Josanie lost one warrior. This was through a region patrolled by eighty-three companies of United States troops.

Swallowing pride, Captain Bourke and a handful of perceptive fellow officers grew to respect and praise their opponents. One Apache tactic was invariably successful, wrote Bourke. "A number of simultaneous attacks were made at points widely separated, thus confusing both troops and settlers, spreading a vague sense of fear over the territory infested, and imposing upon the soldiery an exceptional amount of work of the hardest conceivable sort.

"He is fiendishly dexterous in the skill with which he conceals his own line of march. . . . He will dodge, twist and bend in all directions, doubling like a fox, scattering his party the moment a piece of rocky ground is reached. . . .

"The Apache was a hard foe to subdue, not because he was full of wiles and tricks and expert in all that pertains to the art of war, but because he had so few artificial wants. . . .

"It was this peculiarity of the Apaches that made them such a terror . . . had compelled the King of Spain to maintain a force of 4,000 dragoons to keep in check a tribe of naked savages, who scorned to wear any protection against the bullets of the Castillians, who would not fight when pursued, but scattered like their own crested mountain quail, and then hovered on the flanks of the whites, and were far more formidable when dispersed than when they were moving in compact bodies. This was simply the best military policy for the Apaches to adopt—wear out the enemy by vexatious tactics, and by having the pursuit degenerate into a will-o'-the-wisp chase. . . ."

The vaunted frontiersman fared no better in punishing his tormenter. Take for an example an account of one of the raids made by Apaches, which the Alta California newspaper reported in 1886.

"They raided through the Sulphur Springs Valley into the mountains on this side, killing a well-known rancher. This was duly made known, and a company of volunteers from Tombstone started in pursuit of the offenders. This company were well mounted at their own expense, and provided with food in the same manner. They struck the trail of the Apaches beyond the mining camp of Bisbee and followed it faithfully for several days; their reason for not following it to the end is the same as that which prevents the regular troops of the U.S. Army from overtaking the hostiles, simply because they could not, and why?

"Let us see. The first day they made good progress in lessening the distance between themselves and their hoped-for captives. The second day they had done so well as to see the renegade campfire by evening. The third day they came upon campfires yet burning, and abandoned horses.

"The trail had led for miles along the highest ridges and up and down the highest mountain peaks, down the side of one precipitous mountain only to mount yet another more toilsome. Here and there would he come upon the miserable remains of a horse, which succumbing to the merciless urging of the fleeing redskins, had been made to serve as food. . . .

"Their less ferocious pursuers, unable to draw thus unceremoniously from their steeds for rations, were running short by this time.

"The Apaches have, where opportunity offered, dropped members from their band to take other well-known trails to the Mexican Sierra Madres. The white men therefore find their victims diminished in numbers.

"The whites have not drunk water for a day; the Indians drank generously of the blood of the last horse killed. The civilized white sees his provisions gone; the Indian now shows his crowning superiority. . . .

"The horned toad, loathsome to the civilized man, is not amiss to the noble red. The snake, lying in his path, is shunned by the dainty child of the city; the aborigine scorns not the reptile, but adds it to his stock. [A forgivable error; Apaches for religious reasons would not kill snakes. For dinner, they preferred rats, or best of all, a mule.] Thus, the hardpressed Indian fattens on the road that is bringing famine to his pursuer."

For all its failures, the American army in the field against the Apaches was of high professional order. The generals were experienced and ambitious; the junior officers, of exceptional quality.

"Crawford was born a thousand years too late," a fellow officer wrote of Emmett Crawford, captain, Third Cavalry. "Mentally, morally and physically he would have made an ideal knight of King Arthur's Court. Six feet one, gray-eyed, untiring . . . modest, self-effacing, kindly. . . . His expressed wish was that he might die in the act of saving lives of others." The captain got his wish in a misbegotten brush with Mexican troops.

Enlisted American troops were volunteers to a man: five-year enlistees, with an average age of twenty-three. Many were from the lower social classes but they were well-trained and tightly disciplined.

Frontier service was mean and lonely. Enlisted mess was salt pork, mush, stew, prunes and black coffee. At best the men were quartered in mud or clapboard barracks at places like Camp Grant, "the most forlorn parody of a military garrison in the most woe-begone of military departments." At worst, they were in forced march carrying a heavy single-shot Springfield and 40 rounds of ammunition with nothing to eat but hard bread and rancid bacon.

If a cavalryman, "he was supposed to have a horse; the nomenclature for his position called for one, but it seemed like he always walked." If an infantryman, there was never any question about "endless marches under an unsetting sun."

In a memoire of his late summer 1855 epic march, Lieutenant Britton Davis would write, "In 24 days since leaving the command we had marched over 500 miles through a mountainous country in driving rains, much of the way in mud so deep that the mules sank above their fetlocks. Seldom were we able to ride.

"When I rode up to the door of the commanding officer's office (at Mexican El Paso) just after dark, I was certainly a sight for sore eyes. Ragged, dirty, a four-months' beard, an old pair of black trousers that had been partly repaired with white thread blackened on the coffee pot, rawhide soles to my shoes, and my hair sticking through holes in my campaign hat; who would have accepted my statement that I was a commissioned officer of the U.S. Army? The Mexican colonel in command did not."

The Geronimo outbreak in 1885-86 was in certain aspects the most remarkable guerrilla action in recorded history. Bolting their reservation in Arizona's White Mountains, Geronimo and his band fled 120 miles without food or rest.

Lieutenant Davis reported, "We ascertained later that the hostiles traveled 90 miles without halt. . . . On the trail that day we found two dead babies, newly born."

A group of the Apache scouts who helped track Geronimo

By now the renegades were better equipped than the soldiers. All braves had field glasses. Large-calibre Winchester repeaters were standard. If they couldn't steal ammunition, they manufactured it. They coped with the paleface telegraph with sophisticated sabotage: a snip of wire replaced by a strand of leather— maddening for a repairman to locate.

Geronimo was master of the night march. His men memorized future assembly areas. Rear guards and fake camps were set to delay and dupe pursuers. As public disfavor piled up on General Crook and his troops, a retired army officer went to their defense in a letter to the St. Louis *Republican*. He wrote:

"It is laid down in our army tactics (Upton's 'Cavalry Tactics,' p. 447) that 25 miles a day is the maximum that cavalry can stand. Bear this in mind, and also that here is an enemy with a thousand miles of hilly and sandy country to run over, and each brave provided with from three to five ponies trained like dogs. They carry almost nothing but arms and ammunition; they can live on the cactus, they can go more than 48 hours without water; they know every water hole and every foot of ground in this vast extent of country; they have incredible powers of endurance; they run in small bands, scattering at the first indications of pursuit. What can the U.S. soldier, mounted on his heavy American horse, with the necessary forage, rations and camp equipment, do against this supple, untiring foe? Nothing, absolutely nothing.

"General Crook has pursued the only possible method of solving this problem. He has, to the extent of his forces, guarded all the available passes with regulars, and he has sent Indian scouts on the trail after Indians. He has fought the devil with fire. Never in the history of this country has there been more gallant, more uncomplaining, and more efficient service than that done by our little army in the attempt to suppress the

Geronimo outbreak."

Little as Crook's army may have been, Geronimo's was one-hundredth. Geronimo had thirty-five adult braves and eight boys. With them were a hundred women and children. Their only means of supply were the stores of their enemies. Deployed against them were 5,000 regular American soldiers, 500 Indian auxiliaries, hundreds of armed American civilians, plus a considerable Mexican force, both military and civil.

During four months of 1885 the Apaches killed seventy-five civilians in Arizona and New Mexico, twelve Apaches who were friendly to the whites, two officers and eight soldiers of the American army, and probably more than 100 Mexicans.

Geronimo's lost six men, two half-grown boys, two women, and one child. Not one was killed by regular troops. Only three of Geronimo's warriors were killed in open battle. (Unlike the Americans, Apaches had no system of recuperative leave for the wounded. Geronimo, himself, was shot five times and wounded seriously by saber and rifle butt.)

Not the first time nor the last, army headquarters and presidential administrations in Washington were embarrassed and mystified by the bad news from the front.

"The difficulties of subjugating the Apache were so unique," recalled a troop commander, "that they were not understood even by our superior officers in Washington. No one who had not been through the mill could understand them. General (Phil) Sheridan, at that time in command of the army, was hopelessly at sea in his knowledge of these people, their mode of warfare, or the problem of catching them. His ignorance of these matters led him to give orders that were impossible to carry out."

Peace did not come to the frontier until the army induced hundreds of Apaches to become paid scouts, who tracked, infiltrated, decimated and betrayed their renegade brothers. The scout companies were the inspiration of General Crook who discerned in them double value: it took an Indian to catch an Indian, and an Indian mercenary was one less Indian white soldiers had to fight.

In the field, officer cadres were enthusiastic over their scouts. Captain Dorst said, "My scouts will start at the bottom of a steep mountain, 1,500 feet high, and go on a trot clear to the top without stopping. There isn't a white man alive who could run 50 yards up the same pitch without stopping to catch his wind."

To footsore whites, the toughness of scouts became legend. Newsman Charles R. Lummis once visited a wounded scout in the Fort Bowie infirmary.

"He cajoled a cigarette paper and tobacco from me, which he handled with Mexican dexterity. Then he sat up in bed, kicked his poor wasted legs from under the cover, turned up one caloused foot, and drew one of those torpedo parlor matches across his bare sole. A strip of sandpaper couldn't have been more effective. The match went off like a toy pistol. No use in expecting that sort of foot to rebel at a little inhumanity."

In one last convulsion of ignorance, Sheridan replaced General Crook with General Miles. The scouts were discharged from the service. A puffed-up white supremist, Miles immediately hand-picked teams of the finest Caucasian athletes in his army and mounted them on his soundest horses.

"An experiment to ascertain if the best athletes in our service could not equal in activity and endurance the Apache warriors," said Miles.

Five days after Captain H. W. Lawton picked up Geronimo's trail the cavalry horses were worn out and had to be abandoned. The captain succumbed to exposure and had to be carried on a travois. The net result

In pursuit of Geronimo, May, 1886

of four months of the most agonizing campaigning was the seizure of the ponies and camp equipage of one small band of hostiles. General Miles abandoned his experiment.

Geronimo was never captured. Apache scouts were sent to negotiate. Out of homesickness and longing for loved ones, the renegade chiefs surrendered September 4, 1886, and four days later were put aboard a train for imprisonment in Florida. In one of the blackest injustices in white treatment of Indians, the loyal scouts were imprisoned along with the hostiles, including the two scouts who negotiated Geronimo's surrender. Just as the train was pulling out of Bowie station, the Fourth Cavalry band struck up "Auld Lang Syne."

For Americans with recent experience or current knowledge of Indochina, there are abundant points of reference in the Apache quagmire.

The pithy axioms of old General Crook seem fresh at the moment: "If you have 10,000 troops and one Indian tied down in the middle of them, you don't need an Indian policy."

And, "It is idle to talk of de-tribalizing the Indian until we are ready to assure him his new life is the better one."

And, "To operate against the Apache we must use Apache methods and Apache soldiers." He was an early advocate of "Apache-izing" the war.

The entire program on the frontier Southwest was nearly wrecked by internal bickering, massive corruption, and gross misjudgments.

An inspector-general reported a thriving black market and runaway inflation in Arizona. Army hay cost $60 a ton, grain $12 a bushel, freight from San Francisco $250 a ton. One small fort headquarters building cost $100,000, with an additional $10,000 for the flagpole.

Civilian contractors filled cattle with water before

weighing, then compounded the crime with tampered scales. "Not enough fat on the animals to fry a jackrabbit," an officer complained. Lieutenant L.A. Abbott reported to higher-ups that not half of the $240,000 in supplies purchased in 1877 were ever delivered.

Less than a century later ship-to-shore losses in Saigon harbor were being estimated at forty per cent. "By watching the Saigon black market," a GI commented, "we know what will be on the shelves of our PX tomorrow."

The difficulties of charting progress in a guerrilla war likewise were never solved in Apacheland. In 1883, "body count" was meaningless—"How many had been killed and wounded could never be definitely known, the meagre official report, submitted by Captain Crawford, being of necessity confined to figures known to be exact."

And after another battle, ". . . by the time we had made our way to the top of the rocks the enemy had gone with their wounded, leaving only two pools of blood to show where the bullets had taken effect."

A hawk-dove debate divided America over costs and benefits of the Apache war.

Sarcastically, anti-military pacifists suggested that a federal grant of a fortune to every Indian in the long run would save money, "the annual military expense could be halved." Noting that the cost of fighting Apaches was nearing $50 million, an Indian agent stated, "One-tenth of the expenditures on fruitless campaigns could have provided comfortable homes for all the Indians in the Territory."

Reminiscent of those jibes is the late Bernard Fall's arithmetic regarding Vietnam. By dividing the total number of enemy killed into the total American war expenditure, Fall concluded that it costs an average $500,000 to kill a communist in Vietnam, enough to have made a capitalist out of every one.

In Arizona one general abhorred publically exhorbitant costs. A post of 150 men cost $3 million annually to maintain, he said, adding, "War is the economic base of Arizona Territory."

A press dispatch from Arizona, 1885: "The longer the war can be kept up bloodlessly, with just enough menace to excuse the retention of a strong military force, the better it will suit the commercial part of Arizona."

In the Vietnam war, computers have figured it requires 289 soldier-hours to capture one enemy. The man-hour rate must have been tenfold in Arizona, yet hawkish generals held sway; "Root out, capture and hunt Apaches as if they were wild animals," General Ord decreed. He also passed the word that officers "would be promoted in proportion to their success." In Ord's thinking was genesis of the interminable "search-and-destroy" missions of the 1960s.

Then as now, a vocal segment of the home front cried for a military victory. *The Arizona Citizen* of April 15, 1876, editorialized, ". . . the kind of war needed for the Chiricahua Apaches, is steady, unrelenting, hopeless and undiscriminating war slaying men, women and children . . . until every valley and crest and crag and fastness shall send to high heavens the grateful incense of festering and rotting Chiricahuas."

Press coverage of the Apache campaigns suffered a credibility gap in part, at least, of its own making. From Fort Bowie in 1885, Reporter Lummis filed a dispatch beginning, ". . . the unapproachable and supreme twister of truth's caudal appendage is the fiery, untamed, mouthful Arizonan—the multitudinous gentleman who has been feeding the Associated Press reports of the Apache campaigns. Of these reports I believe it is moderate to say that not one in 15 has been even approximately true."

A few weeks later as his admiration for the cavalry

increased, Lummis wrote, "I would like to see about 200 newspapermen whom I could mention forced to join such an expedition. Their brains might then get rid of a little of their present military flatulence."

Some eighty years later Columnist S.L.A. Marshall would write from Saigon, "Think for a minute! Here is Telestar out in space distributing the phenomena of our day around the world at the speed of light. . . . In Saigon there are 350 correspondents supposedly assigned to making the war and its issues understandable to people, everywhere, a group thrice the size of the press gallery in the Korean War.

"Yet despite all this elaboration the struggle in Vietnam is the most wretchedly reported war in the fane of our history since old Zach Taylor fought at Buena Vista. Never before have men and women in such numbers contributed so little to so many."

Pompous General Miles, who fell heir to Geronimo's final surrender, forecast something of technological warfare. In his first order after succeeding Crook, Miles established twenty-seven heliograph signal stations on Southwestern Peaks.

The announced object was rapid movement of military messages by use of sun flashes. When installed the system could move a message of 25 words 400 miles in two hours. In practice, the heliograph mainly carried General Miles' public relations releases. Not one Indian capture could be attributed to the heliograph; not one battle resulted from its use. Three generations later, in exquisite irony, the army's electronic proving ground at storied Fort Huachuca in Southern Arizona would develop an electronic sensory complex to be installed as a main line of defense between the two Vietnams—a military fixture of such astronomical cost and questionable value in irregular warfare, that the "MacNamara Line" was never finished as originally described.

The enemies of this day, and that, withstand certain

comparisons. The Apache and Viet Cong guerrilla are strikingly similar in physique, stamina and determination. The extreme shame that Apaches felt when criticized by peers was related to Oriental "face." Both opponents will be remembered as fanatically loyal to family units, and fiercely possessive of what they considered home territory. Every plant and animal and turn of the planet had a spiritual meaning to the Apache; for the Vietnamese peasant religion is an omnipresent thing, enveloping all the individual's daily acts.

To be sure, there are differences to be cited as well, in global issues, scale of battle, political motivation, and topography. But no trick of the imagination is needed for reviving the cliche, "The more things change, the more they remain the same."

From which theatre of operations came these stories? "The kid stood stock still, his face frozen in a foolish grin. The thing had come at him out of the elephant grass, nicking his side and burying in the earth. It was a primitive spear, five feet long . . . needle sharp and hard as steel.

"She squatted in the dusty road . . . and cradled his head in her lap. She grieved for him—her wails muted, her body wracked with dry sobs. To us, he was a dead (enemy) guerrilla who got what he deserved. She knew only that he was her man. And that he was gone.

"(The patrol was out a week), they had no enemy body to show for their ordeal. They had not seen the flash of an arm or the bob of a head of anyone fighting them. They were uncertain of the source of the fire that had stopped them and killed some of their comrades. The mystery of the fight would stay with them and so would the solacing thought that they had been, all things considered, lucky.

"Never in history has an army been deployed with more exacting rules of engagement," said Col. Harold C. (Hal) Moore, commander of the Third Brigade of cavalry. "We are obliged to respond to hostility with the absolute minimum of suppressive fire, especially when civilian populations are involved. This costs us casualties."

It so happens that all the dispatches are from Vietnam, by Jim G. Lucas, S.L.A. Marshall and myself. But any and all could have been sent from the American Southwest during the Apache wars.

Geronimo died in captivity, at age 80, at Fort Sill, Okla., in 1909, and at least one Arizonan detected "a sigh of relief the world around." In 23 years of confinement his fame increased, while the reputations of his opposing generals dissolved in bickering for glory.

Are the Apache campaigns truly, significantly relative to this day? An arrogant response is available, "Surely, Geronimo wouldn't have lasted ten days against modern air cavalry equipped with helicopters, massed indirect artillery, and radio communication."

Perhaps not. Although in *their* war the Apaches began with stone age weaponry, and in the end were better armed, equipped and transported than their opponents. The mind reels at the thought of Victorio, Geronimo, Nana, Cochise, Nachite, Delshay, Mangus Coloradas, and Juh (interestingly enough, pronounced "Ho"), in possession of plastic explosives, Molotov cocktails, walkie-talkies, mortars, machine guns and rockets —all acquired in raids of enemy arsenals and stores.

"It is the spirit which wins battles and will always win them," Barbey d'Aurevilly has said, "just as it has won them in all periods of the world's history. The spiritual and moral qualities of war have not changed since those days. Mechanical devices, precision weapons, all the thunderbolts invented by man and his sciences will never get the better of that thing, so despised at the moment, called the human spirit."

Could it be that Geronimo today, in a country he knows and loves, with near sanctuaries in neighboring

The surrender of Geronimo in Skeleton Canyon

weak states, facing opponents of shaky alliances, taking advantage of his foe's corruption, softness, extended supply line, and unfamiliarity with the native population—might not Geronimo frustrate the world's greatest military power for three, five, seven, ten—who can say how many years?

Raymond Friday Locke is the editor of *Mankind,* the magazine of popular history. His book-length history of the Navajo Indians will be published in 1971.

Walter Jarrett has published numerous articles on the American Indians. Recently he was one of the writers selected to develop a textbook for college level American Indian Studies Programs.

Robert Silverberg has authored several books on archaeological and historical subjects, including *The Old Ones: Indians of the American Southwest* and *Mound Builders of Ancient America.*

Lillian Morris and Philip Procter are both of Cherokee descent. They have published in several American and foreign publications.

Norman B. Wiltsey is the author of the bestselling history, *Brave Warriors.* Don Dedera has lived in and written about the American Southwest for twenty-five years and recently has toured Vietnam and reported on the war twice.

Sharon S. and Thomas W. McKern are writers specializing in physical anthropology. Thomas McKern is a professor of anthropology at the University of Kansas.

Robert Easton, one of radio's original "Quiz Kids," is a character actor in films and television. He is currently writing a book on American Indian humor.

Each new issue of Mankind magazine brings you the delight of discovering fresh, bold, unexpected ideas relating to man's adventure on earth. You may join the Knights Templars crusading to free the Holy Land in one article, then thrill to Lord Byron's vision of the glory that was Greece in another. You could visit with Catherine the Great of Russia, travel in the western badlands with Jesse James, explore the London slums of Hogarth's England or battle with Grant at Vicksburg. The writing is lively. The subjects fascinating. The format bold and dynamic. Priceless photographs, authentic maps and drawings and magnificent art in full color illustrate articles written by the world's foremost historians and authors. Mankind is the most entertaining and rewarding magazine you and your family can read. Discover the pleasure of reading Mankind now. Your introductory subscription rate is only $5 for the full 6-issue year.

GREAT ADVENTURES OF HISTORY

These books, produced in the image of Mankind magazine, provided interesting reading on a variety of fascinating subjects grouped to a singular theme in each volume. You will enjoy reading all books in this series and, in addition, find the varied subject matter, the quality production and visual beauty make these books ideal gifts for any occasion.

CURRENT TITLES IN THIS SERIES.......**$1.75 ea.**
- THE ANCIENT WORLD (22-001)
- GREAT MILITARY CAMPAIGNS (22-002)
- THE AMERICAN INDIAN (22-003)
- THE HUMAN SIDE OF HISTORY (22-004)

GIFT BOXED SET OF ALL 4 VOLUMES.......**$6.95**
- ALL 4 BOOKS GIFT BOXED (22-005)